ACTING REFRAMES

D1616253

Acting Reframes presents theatre and film practitioners with a methodology for using Neuro-Linguistic Programming (NLP) as a tool to aid their practice.

Author Robert Barton uses the NLP approach to illustrate a range of innovative methods to help the actor and directors, including:

- reducing performance anxiety
- enabling clearer communication
- intensifying character analysis
- stimulating imaginative rehearsal choices.

The author also shows how NLP can be used alongside other basic training systems to improve approaches to rehearsal and performance.

The book shows the use of NLP to the reader in a playful, creative, and easily accessible style that is structured to enable solo study as well as group work. The text offers a range of engaging exercises and extensive analysis of language patterns used in performance. It is a source for enhancing communication between all theatre practitioners in training, productions, and daily life outside the theatre.

Acting Reframes gives actors a richly rewarding approach to help them develop all aspects of their craft.

Robert Barton is Professor Emeritus of Acting at the University of Oregon, USA. He is the author of *Acting: Onstage and Off*, *Voice: Onstage and Off* (with Rocco Dal Vera), *Theatre in Your Life* and *Life Themes* (with Annie McGregor) and *Style for Actors*. His column "Many Right Ways" appears in each edition of *The Voice and Speech Review*.

ACTING REFRAMES

Using NLP to make better decisions in and out of the theatre

Robert Barton

Routledge
Taylor & Francis Group

LONDON AND NEW YORK

First published 2011
by Routledge
2 Park Square, Milton Park, Abingdon, Oxon OX14 4RN

Simultaneously published in the USA and Canada
by Routledge
711 Third Avenue, New York, NY 10017

*Routledge is an imprint of the Taylor & Francis Group, an informa
business*

Acting Reframes
© 2011 Robert Barton

British Library Cataloguing in Publication Data
A catalogue record for this book is available from the British Library

Library of Congress Cataloging in Publication Data
Barton, Robert, 1945-
Acting reframes: using NLP to make better decisions in and out of the
theatre / Robert Barton.
p. cm.
Includes index.
1. Neuro-linguistic programming. 2. Acting. 3. Performing arts. I. Title.
BF637.N46B37 2011
658.4'063–dc22
2010043558

ISBN: 978-0-415-59231-4 (hbk)
ISBN: 978-0-415-59232-1 (pbk)
ISBN: 978-0-203-82910-3 (ebk)

Typeset in Times New Roman by
Bookcraft Ltd, Stroud, Gloucestershire
Printed and bound in Great Britain by
TJ International Ltd, Padstow, Cornwall

CONTENTS

PREFACE

Introduction

NLP has offered new dimensions to therapy and business, because it can produce instant results. It is a powerful tool. Employed without a strong ethical base, it can be disturbing. It is alarmingly popular in what I call the "manipulator" professions – law, sales and politics – because it so strongly influences choice. But because actors have to make so many choices, it is a natural fit. Because they also have to manipulate audience response to a certain degree, and manipulate themselves into a creative, focused, unfearful state, NLP can provide a great supplement to the acting process. Here it will be presented with ethical guidelines and a constant emphasis on empathic human connection.

When I first heard about NLP, I thought its application to acting seemed obvious and was surprised to learn how few actors knew about it. When I pursued my certification (surrounded by people outside the arts) I came away believing it had the potential to assist the whole theatre process: greatly reducing performance anxiety, helping actors and directors communicate more clearly, intensifying character analysis, stimulating imaginative rehearsal choices, enhancing the run of the show and helping those involved in a production let go when the time comes for it to end. It can help us do theatre better while enjoying it even more. NLP offers innovative adjunct approaches, without claiming to replace any basic training system and without taking issue with any current training customs. It respectfully offers exciting expansions.

Acting Reframes is a book I hope many acting teachers will want on their shelves, but could also be an adjunct text for exploratory course work for a range of college or conservatory acting classes. I teach an Acting NLP course. While this is not a common part of performance curricula, the availability of this text could inspire others looking to add innovative, non-traditional courses to their curricula. This book could be of interest to anyone seeking self-improvement, to satisfy a curiosity about acting, to improve acting skills and, of course, to all students of NLP.

While there are other introductory NLP texts, almost all sadly lack playfulness and creativity. Most are in fact syntactically dense and challenging. This particular text aspires to the opposite.

While there is no text quite like this, the way it provides a connection between NLP and another discipline altogether suggests comparison with books that pair NLP with such subjects as business, health, law, education and therapy, those that take a physical approach such as Laban or Alexander Technique and apply the principles directly to acting, and other Routledge books that take a separate field and connect it to actor training: Philip Zarilli's *Psychophysical Acting* (martial arts), Rhonda Blair's *The Actor, Image and Action* (cognitive neuroscience) and Sam and Helen Kogan's *The Science of Acting* (neuroscience).

There is always interest in a new "way in" regarding acting. Many theatre practitioners have heard of and been intrigued by NLP but have never found the time to pursue it and would be delighted to have it presented within their own discipline. I hope those who recognize my name will assume the book will be practical and useful.

Using the text

Acting Reframes is structured to accommodate the solo reader as well as groups and classes working collectively. Specific suggestions for application are included for those working alone or with others. The book is divided into six chapters, supplemented by a guide for further study, a glossary, various forms to use in self- and character analysis and a sample syllabus/schedule for those considering creating a class in this subject area.

Chapter 1 ("What is NLP?") examines the origins of the field and basic skills for all readers, not just actors, including numerous language patterns which offer ways of being more in touch with what one is actually experiencing and connecting with others more respectfully. It provides a self-study analysis to prepare for engagement in subsequent activities by identifying desires for change, symptoms and resources. Two of the most powerful anchoring exercises for tapping into positive resources are offered.

Chapter 2 ("What is VAK?) covers the most widely recognized NLP component – visual, auditory and kinesthetic (VAK) learning preferences or modalities, providing keys to recognizing those in others and ourselves. It also examines ways to employ submodalities to bring positive experiences into greater prominence and allow negative ones to recede and thus lose the capacity to inhibit or depress.

Chapter 3 ("VAK in theatre") offers VAK, first in self-descriptions of actors and directors with a strong preference for each, revealing specific strengths and weaknesses for each of these, and establishes the value in moving fluidly between all three. It also explores V, A or K as a tool in analyzing characters and developing characterization. Monolog exploration demonstrates compelling available choices, and an original monolog project provides experiences progressing through all three modes.

Chapter 4 ("Reframing") demonstrates the power in placing a different frame around experiences, perceptions and events, to make each work more effectively for us. It offers transformative vocabulary choices, a variety of warm-ups revealing the power of the unconscious mind to move us towards resolution and a recognition of healthy core states. Metaprograms and metalanguage analysis provide personal insights and enhance characterization. The power and process of rapport with a person – both achieving it and breaking it – is presented in practical applications.

Chapter 5 ("NLP scene study") takes the subject matter of previous chapters into intense scripted work, expanding the rehearsal process and ways of revealing character. Exercises explore and heighten subtext, reveal character histories, enrich modality usefulness, shift rapport, find anchors, and further intensify exploration and potential discoveries.

Chapter 6 ("Getting it done") offers various ways to move ahead in rehearsal, in career choices and in everyday interaction, by chunking tasks up, down or sideways. The powerful Core Transformation offers new insights into positive intention. A variety of swift memorization strategies are offered, along with ways of using presuppositions to help productive action and well-formed outcome strategy to save time before embarking on a important endeavors.

Acknowledgements

I would like to thank my close friend Rocco Dal Vera who, one day long ago, said to me "Have you heard of this thing called NLP? I think you in particular would really, really love it." That motivated me to start studying and he was right. I would particularly like to thank Talia Rogers, my publisher. In the middle of a lunch meeting regarding some other books, the conversation somehow turned to NLP and she suddenly said "Oh my god, you must write us a book on NLP!" That started things rolling and Talia's input has been invaluable throughout the process.

I received the contract offer while teaching "NLP for Actors," which then became a kind of testing ground for exercises which have ended up in the text. I wish to thank my students Sam Greenspan, Jonathan James, Colin Lawrence, Rebecca Learman, Kathleen Leary, Mark Mullaney, Marla Norton and Christine Rattigan for their enthusiastic assistance in this development process. Respondents to the prospectus and sample materials included David Rose (Director of Coaching and Training, NLP for Actors, UK), Ed Hooks (Freelance Actor Trainer), David Krasner (Head of Acting, Emerson College) and Brigid Panet (Associate Teacher of Acting and Director of the Royal Academy of Dramatic Art, RADA). Thanks to Niall Slater for swiftly and efficiently shepherding the project through various stages.

And finally my eternal gratitude to my own NLP teacher, the amazing and inspiring Lindagail Campbell, Director of the Oregon NLP Institute.

1

WHAT IS NLP?

N.L.P. is the most powerful vehicle for change in existence,
whether it is applied to business, law, medicine or therapy.
Psychology Today

Neuro-Linguistic Programming (NLP) is also the most exciting
aid for acting I've run into in many years.

Origins, definitions

NLP was developed by a linguistics professor and an information
scientist, who examined great communicators to figure out what
they all did in the hopes that their interactive excellence could be
transferred. The result is a system that helps us learn how others
code their experiences in order to connect with them better. It
also helps us recode our own experiences in order to feel greater
contentment and to function more effectively in the world.

The name breaks down as *neuro* (brain and nervous system),
linguistic (spoken and unspoken language), *programming* (repeat-
able patterns). Or using *words* to get yourself and others to *respond*
in a productive way *more often*. There are over 100 NLP institutes in both the U.S. and the U.K., and a similar number scattered around the globe. The founders, Richard Bandler and John
Grinder, started with the brilliant research question "What can we
learn from the best communicators that we can apply in our lives?"
Or, as Bertolt Brecht once put it, how can we "steal from the best"?

They decided to examine world-renowned therapists who had brought healing and contentment to thousands of others. They studied Virgina Satir (family counseling), Fritz Perls (gestalt therapy) and Milton Erickson (hypnotherapy), all creators of powerfully innovative ways to restore wellness that were eventually integrated across the therapy community. Virginia Satir could take a family, no matter how dysfunctional, and bring it back into loving accord. She was the first in her field to recognize the value in meeting with each family member separately, helping each to dissolve some resentments before bringing them all together – when they were ready to connect again. Fritz Perls changed counseling by emphasizing the fact that the mind and body cannot be isolated and must be treated together. He encouraged everyone to "Be who you are and say what you feel, because those who mind don't matter and those who matter don't mind." Milton Erickson pioneered the concept of various levels of trance states, connecting with the unconscious mind, the potential for positive change to take place while in a hypnotic state and the importance of being strongly motivated. One of his classic statements was "A goal without a date is just a dream." Like many communication geniuses, their ideas now seem to us like common sense, but all were controversial and innovative when they were first released into the world.

Because all three could "cure" clients so swiftly, many considered what they did not just therapy but magic. But Bandler and Grinder recognized that there were identifiable patterns and structure in their models' actions. They ended up titling their first two books on the subject *The Structure of Magic I* and *II*.

While their approaches were strikingly different, what Satir, Perls and Erikson shared was a use of words that were highly specific and deeply respectful of their clients. They were able to recognize how the people they worked with processed information and to join them, putting them at ease before pacing and leading them in the healing process. They framed ideas in very specific and learnable ways. They reframed their clients' experiences, even the most painful ones, in a way that made those events bearable and allowed them to move forward. They were able to get them to recognize swiftly where past actions had been nonproductive and to embrace useful alternatives.

Using these three geniuses as models, Bandler and Grinder developed a series of exercises that became NLP. Ironically, because Neuro-Linguistic Programming is all about clarity, many have criticized the name as quite the opposite, always requiring considerable explanation for anyone being exposed to it for the first time. Sometimes called "the study of excellence transference" or "software for the brain," NLP is about using *language* to *program* yourself to *respond* more often the way you want to, avoiding knee-jerk, habitual, self-defeating reactions, and being in a place of readiness and productivity. The idea is that we have all been given a brain, but not an instruction manual. Not surprisingly, practitioners almost exclusively use the initials rather than the full name, many referring to themselves as NLPers (pronounced "nelpers") and "verbing" the term as in "He was confused so I NLPed (nelped) him."

While private institutes abound, NLP has not been embraced by the traditional therapy community nor by academia's behavioral science departments. These have historically insisted on a theoretical base that is then tested by a wide range of empirical research to substantiate hypotheses. NLP leaders have always insisted there *is* no actual theory, that the entire discipline is pragmatic and based on "what works," and that its highly personal applications do not lend themselves to control groups, systematic variables and large population research. I am a big advocate of empirical research, but I appreciate this stance and the courage to take it, because of my own experience attending and leading workshops. Every single time I have led an NLP class, the participants report back the very next session that they found immediate applications in their own lives, were able to change their perceptions and choices in an effective way, not necessarily for everything we covered, but always for some. So NLP practitioners feel little need for further substantiation, as they have done mini-empirical research in their own lives and are satisfied with the results.

Nevertheless there is a great deal of criticism of NLP just as there is a great deal of advocacy for it. The confusion often stems from the fact that there are literally hundreds of processes, which are not taught the same way at various institutes or even described in the same way in various documents. In this book, I will attempt to share what, in my own experience, have been the most reliable and worthwhile of the myriad explorations that can fall under the vast umbrella of NLP and to filter these through the life and work of the actor.

Skills

Through studying NLP, the following skills are likely to increase significantly:

- sensory acuity (more readily recognizing shifts of state in others and in yourself)
- rapport (assisting others – and parts of yourself – to feel safe and trusting)
- internal state management (feeling and perceiving by choice)
- chunking (placing tasks into forms and sizes that will get the job done)
- well-formed outcomes (setting goals that are obtainable and clearly planned)
- modeling (recognizing and implementing the learnable patterns of outstanding work)
- resourcefulness (having other choices always available and knowing when to change).

We will address in subsequent chapters ways to achieve each of these skills and states.

Calibration and congruence

These two C words capture benefits of studying NLP. Calibration is the process of noticing and adjusting. It is measuring, comparing, specifying and seeking accuracy. Someone who calibrates well possesses a high level of sensory acuity. So many of us go through life relatively sight-, sound- and sense-impaired, failing to pick up on all the signals around us. Or we may notice, but fail to adjust. NLP gives us more awareness and choice.

Most of us are accustomed to the negative use of congruence, with something described as incongruous. Some words are almost always used in their downside. When was the last time you heard someone called "couth"? Or heard the weather person announced that tomorrow's weather would be "clement"? Incongruous means not quite right, pieces not fitting together, a lack of harmony or agreement. A person who is incongruent may say one thing but do another, lacking self-knowledge, trustworthiness or sense of balance. Someone congruent seems in balance and accord, fully integrated and consistent, while at the same time flexible. When Dr. John Grinder was asked what characteristics he was looking for in his NLP training staff, he answered "congruence" and provided this list of what that state should entail:

1   personal integrity
2   a deep, bottomless curiosity
3   a driving desire to discover new patterning
4   a deep commitment to creating new insights
5   a continuous seeking for evidence that one is mistaken in every aspect of their personal and professional beliefs
6   an open-learner attitude to exploring life
7   a desire to be of service
8   a commitment to physical health fitness
9   real-world experience in any field in which one intends to present NLP
10 an excellent sense of humor.

I don't know about you, but that is the kind of person I want to be. And while I am still seeking, I can offer ready testimony to being closer than ever would have been possible prior to studying NLP.

The two also have a definite relationship: the more we automatically calibrate, the more we are able to stay effortlessly congruent.

Core language patterns

NLP has had a profound influence on everyday conversational choices, many of which have gone into popular usage without our even being aware of their origins. Listening carefully to ways in which the three original models used words, and then noting effective language choices by others, evolved into these patterns. Each of the choices below offers greater clarity of expression than the alternatives and is respectful of other persons involved.

1   Use the exact right small word to describe your experience. Say "and" instead of "but," when you are truly in a quandary. Not "I love you but I am really angry at you right now" but "I love you *and* I am really angry at you right now." In the former case, "but" tends to cancel out the statement before it. If you are genuinely divided and experiencing a dilemma, "and" more accurately identifies your feelings.

If you are in a situation where you are feeling powerless, instead of saying something like "This kind of thing makes you feel like you have no idea what to do," stop and realize that not everyone would feel this way, that in fact the only person you can really speak for is yourself. So replace "you" with "me" and "I" so you are accurate. The tendency to use "you" or "someone" instead of "I" or "me" dissociates you from the experience (see Chapter 2) instead of allowing you to own what you feel.

2   When you need to confront others about something unpleasant that is getting in the way of your relationship, instead of directly blaming them and potentially putting them on the defensive, stay with a factual identification of the connection between their behavior and your response. Telling someone they always make you angry or never respect you or intimidate you, assumes too much about their intentions and power. Instead say "When you do ..., this is what happens for me." You are starting out with what you know to be true, which is free of accusation and is a far more effective way to open a challenging conversation where you are hoping something will change.

3   When you are not 100 percent in a belief, feeling or desire, say "a part of me ...." It is far preferable to acknowledge that you only believe, feel or want something part way, if that is accurate. It is perfectly acceptable to acknowledge two or more parts of yourself that are currently at odds as you struggle toward a decision. This also alerts others that you have not yet made a decision, in spite of their impressions.

4   Too busy to talk with someone but they are in need? Say something like "This needs 100 percent of my attention. I can't give that now, but promise to when ..." Acknowledge the importance of their problem and make a future commit-ment. This is far preferable to brushing them off or strug-gling to give them what they need when you simply cannot do that right now without disappointing.

5   Give someone who did not nurture you or the friend to whom you are speaking the benefit of a doubt. Statements such as "She did not have the skills to give me what I felt I needed" or "You grew up in an era that was ignorant about ..." are ways of creating some small measure of empathy for the oppressor. It is very rare for someone to calculat-edly decide to make our lives miserable. Instead they have usually come from a place of (admittedly hurtful) ignorance. Acknowledge that if the person had known how to do better, they may well have done better, which is often the case.

6   Use metaphor over direct criticism. For example, instead of telling someone directly they are over-reacting, try some-thing like "Wow, that seems like a gourmet reaction to a drive-through" or "a Velcro response to a Teflon issue." Most listeners are able to grasp and accept criticism, softened and yet clarified through metaphor, because it is delivered by association, comparison and resemblance, rather than by sledge hammer.

7   State questionable characteristics in the most positive way possible if addressing the possessor of said characteris-tics, such as "You have a highly developed ability to take a position and stand firm on things." Almost all behavior can be useful under some circumstances and, just as meta-phor ameliorates, so does reframing the habit (clearly the

7

person above is considered stubborn) so that it does have an acknowledged up side. There are times when we want someone like this on our team, who will not give up. Having recognized this, you may then have an opening to add "But it doesn't always work out for you."

8   Instead of saying someone's suggestion is wrong, try saying "Help me understand how that could bring us closer to our goal." You are not jumping on them and are giving them the opportunity to enlighten you. While you may feel the idea sucks, lead with acknowledgement that you may simply not understand yet. Often the other person, when given the responsibility of articulating its value, will himself recognize the idea's fallibility.

9   When being strongly criticized, remind yourself that many people would not even bother to take the time to offer criticism or any feedback at all. Many would take the easy, non-confrontational way out. Acknowledge the effort given and also your inability to respond rationally at this moment. Try "Thank you for noticing me" or "I appreciate your caring enough to take the time to tell me" or "This is something I need to hear" and then add "But now I need time to process it before talking about it further."

10 State what you are seeking or aspiring to rather than what you are avoiding or fearing. Not "Please dear God don't let me get involved with another jerk like that" but something like "Let me find someone who is reliable, compassionate, funny and warm to have in my life."

A few years ago a book and DVD called *The Secret* took the world by storm, staying on the bestseller lists for a record length of time. Ironically, it was nothing more than a recycling of NLP-based concepts, particularly number 10 on the list above, that had been around for decades, and a repackaging of an even older concept called the Law of Attraction. This law can be summed up in two rhyming lines: "What you resist persists" and "Energy goes where attention flows." Number 10 is one of the rare principles that unites both the spiritual and scientific communities. Quantum physics research and spiritual leadership are in complete agreement that we send out and beckon to fields of energy, and that the universe only picks up on our preoccupations. In the case above, it does not pick up on "not a jerk," but rather just "jerk," which is what you are dwelling on. So guess who shows up at the door? Another jerk. If you are dealing with financial issues, instead of constantly saying "I need to get out of debt" (universe only hears "debt") try "I am striving to achieve financial freedom." In these instances, language really does shape experience.

In the past decade a branch of psychology has aimed "to find scientific understanding of thriving individuals, families and communities," with the First World Congress on Positive Psychology taking place in 2009. The field focuses on mental wellness instead of mental illness, replacing the study of psychosis, distress and disorder with the study of optimal experience, positive well-being and engagement. With all due respect, this has been the focus and emphasis of NLP for decades, with studies based on the belief that we can learn more from those who are truly working than from those who are broken.

The NLP apology

In addition to the language patterns above, NLP has also provided us with clear and complete ways of saying we are sorry. Quite often a simple sorry is inadequate if you have really messed up and a complete mea culpa is needed. When you are utterly responsible, try the NLP complete three-part apology:

"I am so very sorry."
"This was entirely my fault."
"How can I begin to try to make it right?"

Do save the above, however, for when you know you blew it. When you are *not* convinced it is all your fault, but are attempting to make amends, try "I'm sorry ..." followed by "for my part in this" or "for the misunderstanding I helped create" or "for whatever I did or said that seemed insensitive."

Levels of competence

As we move along the learning path, NLP teaches that there are four phases through which we are likely to pass. It is vital not to get discouraged, because the first three are temporary if we hang in there.

1   *Unconscious incompetence*: what you are doing isn't working and you aren't consciously aware of it.
2   *Conscious incompetence*: what you are doing still isn't working, however, you are now aware of that.
3   *Conscious competence*: you have deliberately chosen to do it differently now, to get the results you want, and it's starting to work.
4   *Unconscious competence*: it no longer takes a deliberate effort or a conscious choice. The things you have learned are now such a natural, integrated part of you that they just naturally happen – gracefully, effectively, and easily.

Often students begin actor training, thinking they are far more skilled than is the case as in step 1 above. Then they discover just how much they really have to learn and go into step 2, an undoubtedly depressing phase where some will feel completely overwhelmed and give up. However, if they stay the course and apply themselves, they will eventually enter 3, with some sense of accomplishment. They are beginning again to feel some acting skills, but this time with evidence instead of ignorance. The problem with phase 3 for actors is that their work now feels self-conscious, studied, perhaps overly technical and lacking in spontaneity. They are applying the new knowledge but not in an automatic, seamless way. This is the phase that requires patience and dedication, because eventually step 4 will emerge and acting will become natural and free-flowing.

Some performing artists who are gifted (and fortunate enough to skip the first competence phases) avoid training altogether lest they lose the magic, when the likelihood is that, in risking step 3 for a time, the magic will return, multiplied, backed by even greater skill and more reliable access to excellence.

NLP self-study form

When I was first studying for NLP certification, I found that when an exercise came along and I needed to dig into my experience to take part in the activity at hand, I would often draw blanks. Suddenly I could not recall my most important resources, problems and issues. Or I would quickly choose one and then later wish I had picked a different one that mattered more to me. If you take the time to privately fill in the answers to the following questions, instead of my experience, you will have a wide range of choices readily available and greater clarity as to which you wish to choose. (The self-study form is in Appendix A.)

Changes

- Times you felt powerless and clueless:
- Times you felt totally capable and competent:
- Mildly unpleasant memories where you were not at your best:
- Mildly pleasant memories where you were at your best:
- People with qualities you would really like to emulate:
- Something that doesn't really matter any more, but used to matter a lot:
- Something from your past that keeps raining on your parade:
- Someone you wish to stay in love with or get closer to:
- Someone you wish to forget or feel less concerned with:
- Changes you would like to make:

  - Internally:
  - In one-on-one relationships:
  - In groups:

Symptoms

- Habits/addictive behaviors you wish you could break:
- Habits you wish you could acquire:
- Phobias:
- Allergies/repeated illnesses:*
- Traumatic memories:

11

- Knee-jerk responses:
- Circumstances where your buttons get pushed:

(*It may seem odd that a physical malady appears on the list. This is because some illnesses, particularly allergies, are the result of a one-time phobic response on the part of the immune system. Once this response is reversed, some of the physical symptoms dissolve.)

Resources

- Your most rewarding performances:
- Times when you felt fully joyous:
- Times when you felt truly inspired:
- Times when your comfort zone suddenly greatly expanded:
- Things you do as well as anyone:
- Things that are easy for you and difficult for others:
- Perfect moments you've experienced:

Take some time to fill out the form, temporarily skipping over answers that do not come easily, but coming up with enough changes, symptoms and resources to give you raw material for exercises coming up in this and subsequent chapters.

Anchors

An important part of NLP is understanding and maneuvering through the various anchors in our lives. The same way an anchor keeps a boat in place, our life anchors keep us responding the same way to stimuli. Many of the self-study categories are ways of identifying your own anchors. They can be positive and negative. If someone abused you as a child, you may have actually shut that experience out of your consciousness. Nevertheless, if the abuser always approached you by touching you gently on the elbow, whenever that happens now you may freak. Anyone touching you there may cause you to break out in a sweat, to panic and need to move instantly away from the toucher even if you do not know why. The content may have been shut out of your memory, but the anchor is firmly in place.

If you wore a certain color on what was the best day of your life, every time you see that color anywhere you may feel a radiant sense of satisfaction. If you walk into a bakery, the smell of freshly baked bread may transport you instantly and momentarily back into your grandmother's kitchen many years ago and fill you with feelings of warmth and nostalgia.

Have you ever had the experience of visiting someone's home, sitting in a chair, and sensing that everyone was suddenly uncomfortable because, as you eventually learned, that chair belonged to the head of the household and no one sat there even when he was absent? Our lives are full of anchors and the challenge is to create positive ones that us allow us to return to our most productive, satisfying states.

Two exercises in stacking positive anchors follow.

Exercise 1: Piece of Cake

1   Refer to your self-study form for things that are easy for you – things that are challenging for others but just seem to flow when you do them. These do not need to be monumental accomplishments. You may have certain small motor skills or some athletic prowess that you have observed many others do not. You may always have success cooking a certain dish that others find challenging and unpredictable. You can swiftly solve a certain kind of puzzle or predicament that leaves quite a few other people paralyzed.
2   Stand with two imaginary circles on the floor in front of you; the circles have diameters of 2 to 3 feet and one is slightly to your right, the other to your left.
3   Pick something you do well and easily. Step into the circle to your front right, remember fully and enjoy the satisfaction that it gives you, noting how it looks, sounds and feels. Bask in the pleasure of that accomplishment as you snap your fingers and say "Piece of cake!"
4   Step back into your initial position, leaving the full sensation of easy achievement in the circle.
5   Repeat this process with other skills, at least two more and up to a half dozen. Always remember the sight, sound and

feelings involved. Let each new "cake" sensation join the others rather than replace them. Each time you load the circle again, you are stacking positive anchors.

6 Stand in the circle with all the mellowness surrounding you and the skills commingling, savoring the various ways in which you are able to "let it be easy" in a number of contexts. While full of this kind of satisfaction, think of a future encounter that offers challenge. This may be something you experience frequently where you never feel quite satisfied with how it went – something you may not handle well, that *should* be easier than it is.

7 Place that encounter in the circle to your front left. Armed with all the anchors from circle right, imagine approaching the future event, literally walking in the door or driving up, going through the activity, but more easily, breezily and fluidly than ever before, letting it be far easier than it has been in the past.

8 Filled with resources, step into the left circle and visualize yourself fully in the future encounter, snapping your fingers again and saying "Piece of cake!"

9 Step back into the right circle again, enjoying your easy accomplishments. Plan on taking this easy-going energy with you to the actual event.

10 Step back into the neutral space again and savor the comfort and freedom with which you will approach the forthcoming/ recurring challenge.

This exercise is a great reminder of how much the success of an encounter is influenced by the attitude brought into it. It also shows that small skills, when stacked together, can create power. Do all subsequent encounters go extremely well? No. But what almost invariably happens is that the event loses heat or the capacity to preoccupy and inhibit. Whatever happens is easier to take.

Exercise 2: Circle of Excellence

1 Use the self-study form and your memories to pull up the moments of triumph or major accomplishment in your life, times when there was a genuine challenge and you rose to

the occasion. These are very different from the previous exercise, because no one would ever claim that they were easy. You may have had to study long and hard, to rehearse and experiment with every fiber of your being, to push the limits of what you thought you could do. You set out to be better, finer, sharper, more fully evolved than you had been and you did it. When you swell with pride, these are the moments you remember.

2 Place in front of you an imaginary circle at least a yard in diameter.

3 Step into the circle and relive the extraordinary pride, relief and feeling of achievement in one of your significant accomplishments, loading all the sights, sounds and feelings (physical and emotional) that were present. If there were distinct smells and tastes involved, because these are powerfully evocative, load them in as well. Make the memory as strong as possible. Savor it. Relish it fully.

4 Step back into neutral having loaded all the sensations in the circle.

5 Select other triumphant moments and repeat the process several times, again step by step, stacking resourceful memories.

6 Stand in the circle allowing these various memories to coexist and blend, filling you even more with a sense of excellence that has been present in your life, joyous in your own demonstrated capacity to rise to occasions.

7 Step back into neutral and proceed to furnish your circle. Like a decorator with an unlimited budget and a wizard with unlimited magic, make selections that are so attractive to you that you will eagerly return. At each stage below, make a decision outside the circle, step in to test if that is what you really want and adjust it as desired.

- What do you want the border of the circle to be like? A giant golden ring, a circle of your favorite flowers, a whirling breeze?
- What do you want the actual inner circle to be like and feel like? Cool marble, grass, deep carpeting?

- What would you like to see and experience beyond the confines of the circle when you stand inside? Floating gauze curtains through which butterflies can be seen circling? A circle of fountains with an orchard of willow trees beyond?
- What would you like to imagine when you look straight up above you? Stars? Clouds? A canopy? Angels?
- What is a scent you would like to associate with your circle of excellence? Or is there a combination of pleasant, evocative odors you would like?
- Is there a taste sensation you would like to add?
- How specifically do you feel physically when you enter? Cooler? Warmer? Bathed in light? More solid and strong? More buoyant and light?
- What sounds do you wish to hear when you enter? A trumpet fanfare? Heavy metal rock? Tinkling chimes? Thunderous applause and cheers?

8 Let your imagination fill in every sensation possible and promise yourself to continue adjusting these at a later time until they are perfect. Once you have made some basic decisions, it can be great fun to refine your decorating decisions as you drift off to sleep at night or go for a walk.

9 Standing in your circle, fully loaded with experiences of excellence and irresistible décor, select a future encounter that is going to be a real challenge and that will need your full complement of skills.

10 Imagine yourself approaching that encounter, surrounded by your circle, past accomplishments and a full range of sensory stimuli.

11 Determine how you would like to access the circle. Do you wish to walk into it and carry it forward with you? Or would you perhaps prefer it to drop down around you from above? Or to turn on its side as a round entrance that then settles around your feet once you are inside? Experiment with the access mode most appealing to you.

12 Future-pace by creating the exact space, persons involved and circumstances of the upcoming challenging encounter.

Move towards the door or whatever entrance you associate with this encounter, accessing your circle en route and
sensing fully how the event will go with this aid surrounding
you.

13 Step back into neutral, secure that you will be able to employ
your circle when you need it.

These two exercises are similar in that past positive memories
and accomplishments are being stacked to assist you in future
encounters. They are different in that Piece of Cake is useful in
circumstances that you know you could allow to be easier if you
would just get out of your own way. Circle of Excellence is for
challenges that are not easy and require all your resources of
courage, imagination and clarity.

Because actors have so many circumstances where they need to
just get out of their own way and let it happen, and in which they
need to face their fears, dig deeper and shoot for triumph, both of
these processes can be useful. Having said that, which one should
you use with a big audition? I would say, if it is a *prepared* audition, where you have absolutely done the work, you really know
your material, have run it successfully and shared it with others
to positive response, where you know you *should* do well and the
only fear you have is fear – select Piece of Cake. While the occasion is important, what you need most when you are presenting
material that is mastered, polished and theoretically ready, is a
sense of ease and a dropping away of nervous tension that can so
often sabotage actors. Because everyone wants to see actors who
are comfortable onstage that is what you probably need most as
you approach the audition.

On the other hand, if you are in a callback situation where you
may be asked challenging interview questions or put in improvisation situations requiring considerable imagination, I would
consider switching to Circle of Excellence – the reason being
these challenges are not familiar and may benefit from a higher
sense of summoning untapped skills. If you are literally being
pitted against other actors in such a way that each of you does
the speech, dance routine or character encounter one after the
other, where you experience exactly whom you will need to beat

for the role, Circle of Excellence may help you dig out what you need to give you the edge you need. You can do this in a way that allows you not to focus on defeating others, however, but rather on rising to your absolute personal best. Of course, if an audition moves through various stages over a period of time, you may elect to switch back and forth depending on what you feel you need at any given phase.

Both these exercises are vivid examples of processes that characterize NLP, in which past resources are gathered to help in future encounters.

Using this material

Throughout the rest of this book, two alternate approaches will be offered:

ALONE: If you are reading and working by yourself, suggestions are offered for solo experimentation.

GROUP: If you are part of a class, a seminar, or just two or three people reviewing the text together, ways to share exercises and learn from each other are presented.

If, as processes are introduced, no distinction is made between alone and group, the exercises work equally well if you are going solo or simply finding your own isolated space in a group setting.

The skills covered in this chapter are not unique to actors, but would serve anyone wishing to be more effective in the world at large. What makes them particularly valuable for actors is because, perhaps more than the practitioners of any other discipline or profession, they are constantly faced with extraordinary communication challenges and pressures. From the potential terror of auditioning before a show even begins rehearsals through to the equally daunting experience of critics, who have the power of libel, evaluating them publicly after the show opens, actors must constantly face their fears. Interfacing effectively with all the "colorful" personalities involved in theatre can be a minefield – involving massaging egos and proffering difficult requests diplomatically. The perspectives of designers, directors, dramaturges, publicity people, crews, coaches and even other actors can be challenging to comprehend, respect and engage with fully. So finding the right words, beyond those given to you by the playwright, is a constant challenge throughout the process. In helping accomplish all this, NLP can be a great gift.

Summary

NLP was created by observing three of the most brilliant therapists of the past century in action and then modeling their behavior in a way that others could emulate. The challenging name involves using words (Linguistic) to achieve positive and productive responses (Neuro) when you want them (Programming). Keys to success involve calibrating and achieving congruence. Numerous language patterns offer ways of being more in touch with what you are actually experiencing and connecting with others more respectfully. Learning moves through four phases of competence. The NLP self-study form (Appendix A) can prepare you to engage in progressive activities by identifying your own desires for change, symptoms and resources. A key NLP element is anchoring and two of the most useful anchor patterns are Piece of Cake and Circle of Excellence. Material in the text will be adapted to serve equally well those who are working alone or in a group.

Words/names to remember

anchoring
Richard Bandler
calibration
chunking
Circle of Excellence
congruence
core language patterns
Milton Erickson
John Grinder
The Law of Attraction

levels of competence
modeling
Neuro-Linguistic Programming
Fritz Perls
Piece of Cake
rapport
resourcefulness
Virginia Satir
sensory acuity

2

WHAT IS VAK?

It is not the strongest of the species that survive, nor the most intelligent, but the most responsive to change.

Charles Darwin

Many believe that the heart of NLP is VAK. This part is the most widely known element and is employed in mainstream education. Determining whether someone is primarily a visual, auditory or kinesthetic learner and adapting to those preferences, is a widely used tool. There is tremendous power not only in recognizing how others experience the world, but in being willing and able to join them

How do you learn and express yourself?

To help you get a fix on that question, answer the following:

Reflect on how you study:

A   Do you prefer to copy your notes, make charts, graphs, organize the work on the page and take a mental picture of it?
B   Do you retain information best when you're in a study group tossing around ideas, arguing concepts, drilling for memorization?
C   Would you like to move around the room during a lecture, handle and build models, put things together, write notes but

never read them, do a project or experiment emphasizing the idea?

If you were being taught a golf swing, would you prefer to:

A Watch the instructor demonstrate, create a mental movie of the swing and see yourself driving the ball all the way to the hole?
B Have the instructor stand off to the side and call instructions and advice?
C Have the instructor stand behind you and hold the club with you, taking you through the feel of a proper swing?

The best way for a teacher to praise or encourage you is to:

A Smile and write a nice comment on your paper or work.
B Tell you that you did a good job, preferably announcing it to the class.
C Literally pat you on the back.

The most useful tools to help your learning are:

A DVDs, videotapes, power point presentations, films, models.
B CDs, audio cassette tapes, recordings of lectures.
C Simulation games, experiments, projects, "hands-on" and "on your feet" activities.

If you tend to answer (A), you spend at least a considerable amount of time in the visual mode, if (B) auditory, if (C) kinesthetic. How about your language choices? Do you use words like "see, shows, focus, perspective, looks"? When you do, you are visual, experiencing life as a series of images. Do you favor phrases like "tell myself, sounds good, I hear you"? Your world is at that moment highly auditory. Do you say "grasp, handle, hold, feel"? Kinesthetic.

As soon as you know yourself and recognize others, you raise your capacity to connect positively. A visual-learner director may correct a kinesthetic-actor on the pronunciation of a word a thousand times, with great frustration and no success, explaining how it is spelt (because she "sees" the word) over and over. Once she recognizes the actor is a kinesthetic, who will only pronounce the word differently if she explains how it *feels,* she will guide him to move his lips, teeth and tongue into the correct pronunciation positions. Eureka! Communication! The actor pronounces the word right and the director no longer wants to kill him.

An actor with a tendency to work visually will wish to highlight his script and return to looking at the words frequently during rehearsal. An actor with auditory preferences may wish to record and playback often. A kinesthetic needs to get into the right shoes and rehearsal garments and start using props and making contact with others at the earliest possible moment. An effective director will structure rehearsal to include all learning modes. A good teacher will do the same in structuring class and counseling students. A good coach will match modes with an actor. An outstanding actor will work to access learning modes she does not habitually employ, to become master of all three.

A core NLP concept is understanding that, at any given moment, we tend to respond to the world around us in a visual, auditory or kinesthetic way, so that we are experiencing primarily pictures, sounds or feelings. Most of us move through all three modalities at different times and may also blend and overlap categories. Actors, no matter what their original inclinations, will benefit from becoming expert at all three.

Why study modes separately?

If we sometimes change and combine modes, why are we learning them separately?

1   It is far more clear to isolate each modality and fully comprehend it before moving on to combinations.
2   There are enough people who *do* spend much of their lives in a single mode to provide ready observation out in the world.
3   The capacity to switch modes quickly and skillfully depends on being able to isolate them.

4   For improv, comedy sketch and other brief acting forms,
     isolating modalities can be effective, just as the playing of
     archetypes and stereoptypes is, because these short theatrical
     forms require sharp, clear, recognizable decisions. The same
     is true for long forms such as farce and satire where charac-
     ters are more likely to stay within a modality.
5   To benefit from rehearsal experimentation, it helps the actor
     to be able temporarily to go deep into a single mode without
     distraction.

Entering each modality

For the following section:

> ALONE: Read each of the statements out loud and do the
> activity as you read it. If it says your shoulders are raised
> high and tense, raise them and tense them. Add characteris-
> tics one by one, aiming to have all of them in place by the
> time you get to the end of the list.

> GROUP: Sit in a circle and take turns reading a sentence,
> going around the group as many times as it takes to
> complete the list. Imitate the reader physically as she reads
> a line, then repeat what she has said, imitating the line
> delivery and adding comments if you are so motivated. If
> the actor has failed to actually embody the modality, take
> a time-out and offer suggestions and side coaching to help
> her achieve it.

(Consider going through the VAK conjuring warm-ups in Chapter
4 prior to taking part in each of the self-descriptions.)

Visuals' self-descriptions

(NOTE: Some people simply cannot speak as rapidly as high
visuals. If you have to sacrifice something while learning this
modality, let it be tempo, which you can incorporate later once
you have gotten the other patterns down.)

Prelude: Wander around the room, really seeing objects, colors, details for the first time, while cutting off sounds and feelings. Take a moment to experience a world made primarily of images.

I have straight posture and don't understand why others don't.

I sit with my back stiff, often not even touching the back of the chair.

My shoulders are often raised. Okay, some would say I carry some tension there.

I don't move much. Why move for no reason?

I often keep my chin down and my eyes up.

I look right at you.

I crave eye contact. Look at me when I'm talking to you.

My breathing is high and shallow.

Everyone says I talk too fast.

I'm thinking fast and my thoughts come almost faster than I can speak.

People say my voice is sort of a monotone. I'll admit it's high in pitch and often breathy.

I admit to being concerned with appearances and I do like to look good.

I'm very aware of myself from the head up but much less aware from the neck down.

I do like things organized.

I'm neat and orderly, even if I do say so myself. I don't like things untidy.

I'm observant. I notice things.

I'm quieter than the others. I don't see the need for idle chitchat.

I'm usually a good speller.

I memorize through images, pictures. I see things, sometimes I can even see the page turning from something I've read.

I really like charts and lists.

I'm not distracted by background noise.

I have a lot of trouble remembering verbal instructions. In fact, my mind wanders with too much verbal input.

I would much, much rather read than be read to.

Here are some of my favorite verbs: 'see', 'look', 'focus', 'watch', 'show', 'picture', 'reveal', 'notice', 'appears'.

I might talk about 'perspective' or describe something as 'colorful' or 'clear'.

If I take a class, I like to sit near the front, take neat notes, then do lists, graphs, and charts to help me review the material.

I study best alone with *no* interruptions, thank-you.

(TRANSITION: Stop. Stand up and shake out all the (relatively stiff) visual characteristics and energy. Move around a bit, letting all that you have taken on go.

As you wander start humming to yourself at random, segue into humming a favorite tune, then into singing a few lyrics, then imagine hearing your favorite sounds, and select your favorite line from a play or poem to recite, savoring it for all it is worth. If in a group, stop occasionally and share this line with someone before moving on to someone else. Experience a brief connection to a world dominated by sound, before moving back into the seated circle.)

Auditories' self-descriptions

NOTE: Sometimes this modality is broken down into four subcategories:

I am an auditory *digital*. Word choice is important to me. I hate it when someone uses the wrong word. It's all I can do to stop myself from correcting him or her.

I am an auditory *tonal*. Sounds are important. I don't care so much about word choice, but I am *so* offended by gross, ugly noises and voices. I love a deep, rich voice and I can hear instantly if someone is insincere.

I am an auditory *internal*. I have an inner voice. I keep hearing this constant voice, like a tape running perpetually in my head. Sometimes it is my inner critical self, sometimes it's my mother, sometimes my ex, sometimes I'm not sure *who* it is!

I am an auditory *external*. I talk to myself. Well, of course I talk out loud whether someone else is present or not. I work things out, I rehearse for upcoming encounters, I rephrase conversations I've already had. Frankly, I think I have to talk in order to think!

I like rhythm, so am likely to tap my pencil, my foot, my fingers on any surface, searching for or keeping a beat.

I often nod my head as I listen, showing I agree with you or sometimes just to let you know I've heard you.

I may hold or in some way touch own face.

In fact, my hand sometimes moves towards mouth without my even realizing it. I may even partially cover it, if I cannot believe I just said what I did.

I may repeat what you've just said, just to sort of load it in.

Okay, I admit I often move my lips, especially when reading or computing information.

I may sing or hum during an activity.

I like to sit or lean when we're talking.

I may exhale when thinking and may sprinkle my speech with lots of non-verbal noises, sighs, groans, squeals, etc.

I talk to myself.

I am so easily distracted by background noise. I cannot understand how other people can study, talk, *concentrate* with a radio blaring or loud chatter across the room.

I speak easily and am somewhat puzzled by those who seem to have nothing to say.

I really love music, but I want to stop and listen to it. Music doesn't just fade into the background for me.

I'm a pretty good mimic.

You know, I learn by listening.

I favor verbs such as: 'ring', 'buzz', 'tell', 'hear', 'sounds like', 'talk', 'speak', and 'listen'.

I may use musical terminology, terms like 'discord', 'harmony', 'dissonant' to describe conditions in my life.

I like to study with friends, discussing material, reading out loud to each other, and quizzing each other verbally.

I wish there were more oral and fewer written exams in this world!

(TRANSITION: Stop. Stand up and shake out all the (somewhat more fluid) auditory characteristics and energy. Move around a bit, letting all that you have taken on go. Feel your clothes against your body and imagine what it would be like to wear your most comfortable outfit right now. Pick some athletic or dance moves which are your favorites and stop to execute them before moving on. Stop and experience briefly the most intense emotional experience of the last few days, then shake it out. If in a group, wander around making some kind of physical contact, hand shakes, hugs, high fives, chest bumps, some kinesthetic connection with everyone in the room. Then return to the seated circle.)

Kinesthetics' self-descriptions

Okay, I admit it. I live all over the place. I need a lot of room.

People tell me my gestures can be dangerously broad. Hey, I like to express myself!

When I sit, people say I shlump. I lean back and my hips are often far from the back of the chair.

My shoulders are often sloped down or to one side. I like to shift around until I'm really comfortable.

I'm often athletic. I can see others do an activity and *feel* what it would be like to do it well.

If I'm a dancer, I can watch the choreographer do the routine once, maybe twice and I've got it. I don't get it why others have to be shown the steps over and over.

I might also be a couch potato. My physical responses are such an important part of who I am, that I can be driven to be active or just plain trapped into immobility.

I might be a fitness addict or I might be a food addict.

I have the deepest breathing of all three groups, low in stomach area and deep in the diaphragm.

My voice is slower, softer, and often lower pitched than the other modalities.

Sometimes when I talk, I need to ... pause ... Some people say I take GIANT pauses. I don't know ... ... maybe.

So I've noticed I sometimes lose people's attention when speaking.

Sometimes I get so confused or petered out that the endings of my statements just trail away …

I *do* know how to relax and often experience total muscular release. I can be active, but I like to kick back.

I change rhythms easily, moving out of any single pattern and into another. I feel the beat and I go with it!

All right, I must admit I respond to physical reward. I like a hug or a pat on the back.

I touch people. In fact, I've got to watch out that I don't touch them when and where they don't want it. Hey, I'm tactile!

I stand close. I want you nearby if I'm talking to you.

I guess you could say I have a physical orientation to the world.

I move a lot, I may squirm and toss and get restless. I'm the one who really waits for the class to take a break.

I may then alternatively collapse into total stillness. It's kind of like my computer gets active, then goes into downtime, when I can seem almost comatose.

I tend to have large physical reactions to outside stimuli. I stop in my tracks. I collapse when I'm shocked. I jump in the air at great news. I live in space, you know?

Yeah. It's true. I may point when I'm reading. Hey, at least I don't lose my place.

My verbs? Figure it out! I like words such as 'grasp', 'handle', 'hold', 'get it', 'grab', 'catch', 'cold/hot', 'feel', or 'grope'.

I favor words that are intensely sense-related, such as 'soft', 'hard', 'poke', 'touch', or phrases like 'get in touch', 'hit me', 'iron it out', 'run up against' or my all-time personal choice 'raise hell!!'

How do I study? Well, I'm often not the best student, given the way most classes are taught. I try to find non-disturbing ways to move in class, doodling, squeezing a ball, etc. and take breaks to load information.

I try to volunteer to do demonstrations when allowed. I like to pick up and feel samples, and try to transfer ideas into some kind of manual expression.

I learn by doing! Let me build you a model. Let me draw you a map. Let me act out the event. Let me find a way to get *into* the lesson and I'll do fine.

(COOL DOWN: Stop. Stand up and shake out all the (highly charged) kino characteristics and energy. Move around a bit, letting all that you have taken on go. Stretch anywhere you have accumulated tension. Allow yourself to return to your normal physical state.)

If working with others, discuss what you found most challenging about the exercise and farthest from your own comfort zone.

VAK in trouble

An interesting way to consider each modality is to ask "What is the likelihood that someone favoring it might get in trouble, from needing to be disciplined in class at an early age to being convicted later on?"

Visuals are the least likely to do anything wrong, *ever*. Or if they do, they are the least likely to get caught. In fact the term "goody two shoes" probably originated to describe some visuals who never squirm in class, in fact can sit still for hours, never speak out of turn without raising their hands, are likely to write or print *very* neatly, do not get in fights in the playground and generally don't "make waves." Of course this also means that if they are up to something (embezzling? hacking?) no one suspects them and they can get away with things surreptitiously.

Auditories win points on class participation, but may lose them by chatting with their neighbors. The term "chatterbox" unquestionably originated for a high auditory who simply could not shut up, who may answer a question with way more information than is required, who may in fact be so excited to speak that she forgets to raise her hand and just blurts the answer out. Auditories can be hugely helpful in keeping class discussion going but also somewhat "piggy" about giving others the chance to share opinions, liking to dominate the discussion. Auditories have trouble getting away with mischief, because they are often not that good at keeping a secret, since they almost always feel they have to tell *someone* what they're up to.

Kinos are far and away the most likely to be sent to the principal's office, being restless, drifting in and out of paying attention, frequently having trouble controlling their tempers, and generally feeling constrained by the confines of desks and the classroom, unless the class is physical education. Because they are ruled by feelings, both physical and emotional, they can suddenly be overcome by an impulse they find impossible to contain. While I have seen no solid research, I believe that prisons are full of deep kinos, who succumbed to an overwhelming impulse and made a really bad decision, in extreme circumstances being struck with blind fury and the need to kill. When the rest of us say "I could just kill you," it is an exaggeration. But some deep kinos actually could or, more precisely, could not stop themselves.

Kinos on drugs and alcohol can be dangerous because drugs and alcohol block inhibitions and can unleash irrational, uncensored behavior. High kinos already have overwhelming impulses without needing further prodding or permission. Ironically, those of my students who are not at all kinesthetic tend to agree that they use booze and drugs to become more like their kino friends. Much of the time they may be glad *not* to be like them, but then comes Saturday night. They want to feel freer, to cut loose, dance without embarrassment, flirt provocatively, to join the party and let their normal inhibitions fade away.

Predicates

The most reliable way to determine which modality someone is experiencing at any given time is to notice the verbs and other descriptive words they use regarding the subjects of their sentences – their predicates. Some have been identified above, but here is a more extensive list to help you become alert to VAK engagement.

31

Visual	*Auditory*	*Kinesthetic*
Appear	Audible	Bounce
Clear	Babble	Caress
Cock-eyed	Boisterous	Catch
Colors	Buzz	Clutch
Conspicuous	Discord	Cold
Disappear	Dissonant	Feel
Enlighten	Droning	Firm
Far-sighted	Drumming	Fumble
Features	Earshot	Grasp
Focus	Echo	Grope
Foresee	Grumble	Handle
Glance	Harmony	Hard
Hindsight	Hear	Hold
Horizon	Hiss	Hustle
Illusion	Listen	Impressed
Illustrate	Loud	Kiss
Image	Muffled	Luke-warm
Inspect	Mumble	Nudge
Keen	Murmuring	Play
Neat	Pronounced	Press
Look	Noisy	Poke
Observe	Prattle	Sensitive
Overview	Quiet	Sensuous
Perspective	Resound	Soft
Picture	Ringing	Strike
Resemble	Roar	Stroke
Scan	Rumbling	Tender
Scope	Screech	Tension
See	Shriek	Tickle
Show	Silence	Touch
Sketchy	Sound	Vibes
Tint	Squawk	Beside Yourself
Vague	Squeal	Break Down
Vision	Stammer	Cut Up
Watch	Thundering	Dig In
Blind To	Whispering	Get in Touch
Green with Envy	Clear as a Bell	Have a Feel For
In the Clear	Double Talk	Hit me Like a Ton of Bricks
In the Dark	Give a Hoot	Iron Out
Point	Hear From	Keep Your Shine On
Red Tape	Hem and Haw	Rack Your Brains
Seeing Red	In Tune With	Raising Hell
The Whole Picture	Keep Your Ears Open	Ran Up Against
Clarity	Lend an Ear	Rubs Me the Wrong Way
Unsightly	Rings a Bell	

Classic statements

Visual: I see what you mean – We see eye to eye – It appears that… – Now look here… – Aren't you a sight for sore eyes! – We're trying to look after your best interests – I think you have tunnel vision – You have a blind spot – Let's try to shed some light on the matter – I take a dim view of … – In my mind's eye …– Time for a glimpse of reality – The answer suddenly flashed before my eyes – I'd say the future looks bright.

Auditory: That's a lot of mumbo jumbo – We're all asking ourselves… – Oh, that is music to my ears – Hold your tongue – In a manner of speaking… – Don't turn a deaf ear – I'd say we're on the same wavelength – I heard it from her own lips – This is unheard of – I hear you loud and clear – That's all Greek to me – This is clear as a bell.

Kino: I'll be in touch – That really hit home – Let's just take it one step at a time – You are one cool customer – He's a real pain in the neck – Hold on a second – So we reshaped the whole thing – Let me get a feel for it – Get a grip! – We had a really heated argument – I just can't put my finger on it – I just feel it in my bones – Let's keep moving on this – You're pretty thick-skinned – I just can't grasp the concept.

Accessing cues

1 Take a moment to visualize the front door to your grand-mother's home.
2 Imagine what your grandmother would look like with purple hair.
3 Hear your favorite current pop song.
4 Imagine this song as a duet between Susan Boyle and Lady Gaga.
5 Hear an inner voice saying something to you that you often say silently to yourself.
6 Remember the last time you had a relaxing shower or bath, reliving all the comforting sensations.

For the majority of right-handed people (lefties usually reverse the pattern), the eyes will follow this pattern.

1   Visual remembered – re-seeing something you have seen before, eyes up and to left.
2   Visual constructed – creating a picture you have never seen before, eyes up and to right.
3   Auditory remembered – hearing sounds heard before and known, eyes to the left middle side.
4   Auditory constructed – constructing sounds not heard before, eyes to the right middle side.
5   Auditory digital – talking to self, hearing an inner voice, eyes down and to left.
6   Kinesthetic – remembered tactile sensations or emotions, eyes down and to right.

The eyes respond in fairly predictable ways, offering another helpful means of determining the modality of the person with whom you are interacting. If you ask a fairly neutral question such as "How was your vacation?" the listener will show you before speaking if she is recalling what it looked like, sounded like or felt like. If the eyes go up and back and forth, she may be divided between remembered sights and trying to create one for you to understand. If the eyes dart around generally, the listener may be confused or about to lie.

Changing modalities

It is important, not only to comfortably master and enter V, A or K but to be able to quickly switch in order to join your companion or to change when your character changes. These exercises are designed to give you the experience of rapidly dropping one mode and taking on another.

VAK checklist

Use the list below for a quick reminder of the most widely shared physical and vocal characteristics for each modality. Ask yourself if you are incorporating each as you attempt to inhabit these kinds of characters.

V	A	K
Stiff back?___	Relaxed sitting?___	Butt far from chair back?___
Raised shoulders?___	Tapping?___	Sloped shoulders?___
Chin down?___	Head bobbing?___	Massive gestures?___
Eyes up?___	Touching own face?___	Impulsive moves, sounds?___
Intense stare, poker face?___	Repeating self?___	Squirming?___
Arms tight at sides or on lap?___	Humming?___	Changing rhythms?___
High, shallow breathing?___	Mellow vocal quality?___	Getting up, moving around?___
Talking fast?___	Sensuality of speech?___	Acting out experiences?___
Monotone?___	Non-verbal noises?___	Varying volume?___
Conscious of appearance?___	Mimicking others?___	Gigantic pauses?___
Visual aids?___	Distracted by noise?___	Collapsing after big actions?___

ALONE: Try setting up three chairs in a triangle, one to represent V, another A, another K. When you switch chairs, change modalities. Since no one else is determining when you should switch, test yourself. The minute you begin to feel overly comfortable in one mode, force yourself to move swiftly to another. If you don't want to keep switching, simply determine which mode is least comfortable for you and spend some time each day entering and participating in it.

GROUP: Work in groups of three. Sit in a triangle. Assume each of the following situations:

Arguments

Become three visuals arguing over:

- the most beautiful painting in the world and/or
- the best color in the new clothes this year.

Switch to three auditories arguing over:

- the best song now playing in the top 40 and/or
- the most beautiful, expressive word in the English language.

Now try three kinos arguing over:

- who should have gotten the MVP (Most Valuable Player) award last season in the sport of your choice and/or
- the best snack ever.

(NOTE: You don't need to know anything about art, music or sports to play this game. Feel free to make up non-existent painters, singers, players as well as imaginary styles of painting, music or athletics. The idea is to argue with conviction and to enter the modality.)

Fairy tale

Work in groups of 4 or 5.

- Pick a fairy tale.
- The first person selects V, A or K and starts the story.
- When the leader claps, move on to the next person in the circle who will pick a different modality to continue the story.
- Each time it is your turn, select a mode different from the one you did before.

Planning an event

- Pick a much anticipated (and possibly pretend) event such as a wedding, fair, carnival, parade or fund-raising campaign.
- Pick a mode for your initial presentation. Every time the leader claps, change.

(Discuss what it was like to switch suddenly, which modes are most and least accessible to you right now, and which ones were the most enjoyable to inhabit.)

Submodalities

Within the three modalities, we experience distinctions called "submodalities." These move far beyond our experiencing a world of images, sounds, and feelings to subtle and sharp distinctions inside these dominant modes.

Visual

- Brightness (dark to light)
- Size (small to large)
- Color (black and white to Technicolor)
- Action (still photo, slide to motion picture)
- Movement (direction and speed)
- Frame (defined shape to panoramic screen)
- Focus or clarity (unfocused to sharply defined)
- Location (upright, downleft, etc. to front and center)
- Distance (far to close)
- Hue/color balance (dominant shades, combinations)
- Saturation (transparent to opaque)
- Magnification (long shot to close-up)
- Lighting (source, direction, intensity)
- Transitions (cross fades, quick cuts, etc.)
- Variety (flexibility of frame, single to multiple images, split screen).

Auditory

- Pitch (high to low)
- Tempo (slow to fast)
- Volume (soft to loud)
- Rhythm (heavy to light)
- Tone or timbre (harsh to mellow)
- Form (words, sounds, music, percussion, etc.)
- Digital/word choice (formal to slang)
- Continuity (smoothness to interruptions, pauses)
- Location (external to internal)
- Speakers (monaural, stereo to "Dolby" surround)
- Distance (far to near)
- Clarity (garbled/muffled to clear/crisp)
- Contrast (dissonance to harmony).

Kinesthetic

- Temperature (cold to hot)
- Pressure (insubstantial to intense)
- Location (internal/external, head, ear, stomach, etc.)
- Lubrication (dry to moist)
- Movement (still to active, patterns of moves)
- Intensity (all-encompassing to manageable)
- Duration (constant to occasional)
- Depth (surface to deep)
- Weight (heavy to light)
- Proximity (far to near)
- Touch (tactile sensations)
- Texture (rough to smooth)

plus ...

Smell and taste

At one time the olfactory and gustatory modes were considered separately, but have gradually been incorporated into kinesthetic. These are extremely powerful, as all of us know who have suddenly smelled or tasted something that flooded us with memories and placed us instantly back into a place and experience from the past.

For most of us most of the time when there is a continuum in the lists above, we are likely to prefer the choice on the right for our positive, useful memories.

Submodality checklist

When you are reliving a memory, ask yourself the following questions:

Visual

1 Is it a movie or still frame?
2 Is it color or black and white?
3 Is the image on the right, left or center?
4 Is the image up, middle or down?
5 Is the image bright, dim or dark?
6 Is the image life-size, bigger or smaller?
7 How close is the image to you?
8 Is the speech of the image fast, medium or slow?
9 Is a particular element focused on consistently?
10 Are you in the picture or watching from a distance?
11 Does the image have a frame or is it a panorama?
12 Is it three- or two-dimensional?
13 Are you looking down on it, up, from the side, etc.?
14 Is there a color that impacts you most?
15 Is there anything else that triggers strong feelings?

Auditory

1 Are you saying something to yourself or hearing it from other(s)?
2 What specifically do you say or hear?
3 How do you say or hear it?
4 How loud is it?
5 How fast is it?

6   What is the tonality?
7   Where is the sound coming from?
8   Is the sound harmonious or cacophonous?
9   Is the sound regular or irregular?
10 Is there inflection in the voice?
11 Are certain words emphasized?
12 How long did the sound last?
13 What is unique about the sound?
14 Anything else that triggers strong feelings?

Kinesthetic

1   Was there a temperature change? Hot or cold?
2   Was there a texture change? Rough or smooth?
3   Is it rigid or flexible?
4   Is there vibration?
5   Was there an increase or decrease in pressure?
6   Where was the pressure located?
7   Was there an increase in tension or relaxation?
8   If there was movement, what was the direction or speed?
9   Quality of your breathing? Where did it start/end?
10 Is it heavy or light?
11 Are the feelings steady or intermittent?
12 Did it change size or shape?
13 Were feelings coming into your body or going out?
14 Anything else that triggers strong feelings?

Association/dissociation

Each of the elements above can be manipulated to put yourself in a state where you are more content and comfortable. Select from the self-study form a mildly unpleasant and a mildly pleasant memory, ideally a positive recollection that you would like to experience more often and a negative one that you wish you did not think about and re-experience as often as you do. (NOTE: When first learning NLP patterns, it is good to select experiences and issues that are not apocalyptic or staggeringly crucial. These are so loaded that you may simply be too overwhelmed to actually learn the pattern itself. Select something that scores less than 5 on a 10-point scale. Once you have the patterns in place, go on to larger issues.) Go through the checklist above to determine if the pleasant one is vivid and full. Are you right in the middle of the action (associated) or somewhat muted as you watch yourself? And what of the unpleasant one? Alas, many of us have, out of habit, made our debilitating memories too powerful and our enriching, joyous ones too vague and remote (dissociated) to serve as a positive resource.

Memory management

Here is a process by which you can use submodalities to give your nurturing memories greater prominence and your debilitating ones less power.

Take the unpleasant memory and:

1 Turn it into a still photograph.
2 Place yourself in the photo so you are some distance away.
3 Let the color fade to black and white.
4 Let the size of the picture diminish.
5 Have the photo go somewhat out of focus and become a bit blurry.
6 Place it in a flat white frame just like old-fashioned Brownie photos
7 Let it move farther away from you.
8 Diminish whatever sounds you experience so the volume drops.
9 Let all sounds neutralize to faint and indistinct.
10 Place whatever physical sensations or emotions are involved in the photo itself and not in you.
11 Imagine that you have an old photo album. In your mind, place the small black and white picture in it, close the album, place it in a chest of drawers.

In this way, we have dissociated the memory. (NOTE: we did not try to make it disappear, because there might be a time when you wish to examine it. We just diminished its power.)

41

Now take the *positive* memory and:

1 Turn it into a brightly colored film.
2 Let the screen become panoramic so it seems to have no borders at all.
3 Be right in the center of action so you are the camera.
4 Sharpen the focus for maximum clarity.
5 Let the action and movement swirl around you in a way that is satisfying and engaging.
6 Hear any encouraging words or pleasant sounds vividly.
7 Add a sound track of music that may have been playing or simply musical background you really like.
8 Experience powerfully any scents you associate with this memory or would like to add.
9 Do the same with tastes.
10 Savor any physical contact that you enjoyed.
11 Let the pleasant emotions wash over you and fill you with joy.

You can access this recollection in a powerful and immediate way when you wish. In both of the instances above, submodalities were employed to dissociate or fully associate experiences. While this is useful with memories and it is worth going through the process with quite a few of them, it is also something to consider for the future. When you are actually having an experience in the future, immediately ask yourself if you want to recall this event fully or if it is best diminished and stored away. Then you can begin immediately associating or dissociating to place the memory where you want it.

Because acting is an art full of tragedies and triumphs, it can be helpful for you to make a list of your top ten in each of these categories. Then analyze where they are in their capacity to dominate or invade your thinking. As needed, take the failures into out-of-focus, controllable distance. Take the triumphs into fully loaded, colorful vivacity and the capacity to summon them swiftly when you need encouragement.

What am I?

After spending time fully engaged in V, A and K, many of us are still asking the question: "What am I?" While some will readily recognize themselves as "deep" or "high" V, A or K, many of us are fascinatingly variable. Rather than trying to label yourself, a far more valuable set of questions is:

Where am I at this moment?

Under what circumstances do I tend to fall into V, A or K?

Where is the person with whom I am trying to communicate?

and

What is the best way for us to be in rapport?

What am I when?

This exercise invites you to connect, watch, listen, and feel as you move among modalities. Observe yourself over a few days.

Exercise 3

1   When do you enter a modality strongly even if it is not your usual choice? Under what conditions or circumstances? (For example, I go visual when I feel I am under attack or pressured in some way.)
2   How do your perceptions of the world alter, your physical and vocal lives?
3   Take a moment to go back into a circumstance where you believed you shifted to a large degree into V, A or K. Were there particular triggers you can identify?
4   Come up with a statement of a sentence or two that you made under such circumstances or one that would be typical of you in a modality.
5   If you are working in a group, sit in a circle and have those who are willing complete these statements:

I tend to become visual when …

Something I am likely to say is …

Complete one modality and then go on to each of the others. This can help you recognize circumstances and shifts you may have failed to notice before.

6   Practice going back into these states and then dropping them, so you observe yourself in more detail, have ready access, and also begin to let a state go when it is not serving you.

If you are an actor playing a role, ask:

*   What are my character's preferences? What clues do I get from the predicates and described behavior in the script?
*   What conditions may cause my character to switch or blend modes?
*   How does experimenting with VAK open up more possibilities for my interpretation of this role?
*   How does the capacity to change aid in improving relationships between actors, directors and everyone else working on a show?

All readers, consider the questions:

*   How does the work of an actor auditioning for and then playing a part compare to that of a person seeking and performing his designated role in life?
*   How does someone's tendency towards V, A or K cause others to 'cast' them in a certain role?
*   If we are all trying to act our own lives better, how does a knowledge of VAK help us do that?

Small children are highly kinesthetic, as are animals with whom they often feel strongly connected. Then, as their verbal skills develop, they often go through a highly auditory phase. The educational system tends to support this, allowing children to learn through experience, touch and activity, and then gradually encouraging them to articulate their perceptions. However, gradually instruction tends to grow more and more visual, partially because it is an easier mode of learning to control, as jumping and chattering are replaced by silent watching. Because of the dominance of visual training at the upper levels, it is not uncommon for students with strong auditory and kinesthetic inclinations to find genuine success for the first time in acting classes. Actors need to be able to speak expressively and to be in touch with their physical and emotional lives. So the theatre is just waiting to welcome and honor those who are highly connected in these ways.

Summary

VAK is the most widely recognized NLP component in the culture at large. Learning your own preferences and those of the people around you can instantly enhance your communication with yourself and others. While many of us blend modes, it is far more pedagogically efficient to learn each one in isolation in order to clarify their inherent characteristics. It is important to be able to enter V, A or K fully and empathetically, and to be able to switch quickly if necessary. Keys to recognizing the modality of others are their use of predicates and accessing eye cues. Within the modalities are submodalities which can be manipulated to bring positive experiences into greater prominence in our thoughts and emotions (association) and to cause negative experiences to recede and thus lose the capacity to inhibit or depress us (dissociation). It is less important to decide your own modality than to determine where you and those around you are at any specific time. Acting is a field that is highly welcoming of those with strongly developed auditory and kinesthetic inclinations.

Words to remember

accessing cues	kinesthetic
association	modalities
auditory	predicates
digital auditory	submodalities
dissociation	tonal auditory
external auditory	visual
internal auditory	

3

VAK IN THEATRE

If you judge people, you have no time to love them.

Mother Teresa

So far we have examined the three modalities in everyday life as they can be practiced by anyone, with particular emphasis on applications to the life of the actor, but not to the acting process. Now we will apply them to the ways an actor prefers to work and the ways a characterization evolves. How would a strong inclination towards V, A or K influence one's choices from rehearsal through performance? And how can we learn to relate to everyone's choices and to care for all theatre artists strongly, no matter how different they may be from our own?

VAK actor "success" secrets

Imagine that three famous actors have been asked to describe how they work. Before studying NLP, you might not pick up on their preferences, but now note how revealing their statements can be.

ALONE: Fantasize a context, possibly the one below, in which you the actor may have been asked questions about how you work best. Read your answer out loud, assuming all the relevant characteristics.

GROUP: Pretend this is a talk show. Select a host who will introduce three "very famous" guests who are so successful that they have been asked to describe to others how they work. Imagine these are multiple Oscar, Tony, Olivier, BAFTA and Emmy award winners of legendary status and unparalleled success. Give the guests some time to look over their answers (even better the period between two classes or sessions to get comfortable with the material) before calling them up to chairs in front of the room to tumultuous applause. If the group feels comfortable with the idea, ask the "experts" questions after their initial prepared statement. If you are one of the honored artistes in question, feel free to register your disagreement with the other members of the "panel."

Crucial questions

- How do you work as an actor?
- What kinds of approaches help you the most?
- What do you most dislike in the work of other actors?

Visual

(*Reminders* – high visuals tend to be straight-backed, with raised, tense shoulders, a dropped chin, minimal facial expression, few gestures. Speech is often rapid, breathy, high-pitched, uninflected.)

I never see any progress until I know what my character looks like, clothes, favorite colors, hair, make-up and facial expressions. I need to visualize her before I can be her. I love to see the designs so I can get a vision of the whole show, so I love show-and-tell sessions. I look at magazines, paintings, people on the street. I gaze into the mirror and one day I see her! Next, I try to view the world her way. I try to see people and places the way she would. It also helps me to observe a performance by another actor in the role, not that I would *ever* copy someone else, but it is illuminating to be able to

47

picture every moment in the play. The minute I get the script, I highlight my lines – I really enjoy this! – and I often see them when I speak them, what page, where on the page, the page turning, etc. until I replace these images with others. You know, some actors are offended when directors go up onstage and show them what they want in a scene – actually act it out – but I love that! It really helps clarify things for me, especially if there is violent behavior involved. Just show me what you want me to do. If I can see it, I can do it.

Auditory

(*Reminders* – high auditories usually like to sit, tend to touch their own faces, tap out rhythms and may turn their ears toward you when you speak to them. They like to talk, nod often when listening, and may repeat exactly what you've asked before answering. Voices are pleasant and speech is varied.)

I ask myself, right at the beginning of rehearsal when we are still in the discussion phase, still having those lovely, long talks about text and meaning and the purpose of the show, even *that* early, I ask myself "What is my character's sound?" Is her voice strong, weak, deep, light, loud, soft? And I keep trying to hear her, to let her speak to me and through me. When I get that voice, the rest of the character comes very quickly as my body and spirit just seem to follow. It helps me enormously to tape my lines and listen to them in the car. It is also good for me to tape the director's notes. I hate it most when there are distracting background noises in rehearsal. I do not understand how some actors can work under those conditions! I'm totally mystified when other actors get bored or restless during line notes. I *love* to hear about my line delivery and to keep adding nuance, subtlety and shading. And some actors never talk about their characters outside rehearsal! Some don't even want to talk about them *in* rehearsal! Unbelievable!! If I have doubts about the character, I put those doubts into words. I have never found an acting problem that can't be talked out. I'm not real crazy about fight scenes so I especially like to talk those through before actually doing anything that might be risky.

Kinesthetic

(*Reminder* – high kinos need space, gesture big and often, like to be up acting out experiences and feelings, but tend to slump when sitting. Highly expressive and emotionally available, they also may lose the thread of their (or your) main points, so can alternate between energized and comatose. Voices are often low-pitched and kinos often have a speech tendency to mumble.)

Okay, the first thing I do is I fall in love with the character I'm playing, hopelessly, helplessly in love! Then I gradually let her seep into my bones and crawl into every pore of my skin until she becomes me and I become her. We share a heartbeat! It feels like giving birth! There's pain and struggle, then release and fulfillment Whew!! Whoa!! The best rehearsals for me are when we are *finally* up on our feet and sometimes it seems to take forever to get to that moment. Once I get props in my hands, rehearsal clothes on my body – oh, the right shoes, the feet have got to feel right! – and I can touch, I mean really connect with, the other actors, it all begins to happen for me. I hate rehearsals that are talk, talk, talk, analyze, analyze, analyze, blah, blah, blah … Okay, maybe I don't read as much as I might about the character and play's background, whatever, but I will try *anything* in rehearsal! Oh, and I hate actors who always put off everything: "We'll do the kiss later" or "Don't really hit me; I'm not ready." Shit, I'm ready! I also don't like actors who don't seem to feel things, deep in the gut. That, to me, is not acting!

Again, we recognize that many actors do not fall into these categories, but enough do that you should instantly recognize people with whom you have worked and whose process may have puzzled you. You may have even found them irritating if their choices were extremely different from yours. One of the great benefits of comprehending VAK is that it gives you empathy. You understand that others are simply experiencing their own filter on the world and proceeding as best they can, given their own perceptual limitations and inclinations. The more fluid your mastery of VAK, the greater your capacity to collaborate with a wide variety of performers.

The question inevitably arises "Is one modality preferable to others?" and the answer is no, because each tends to lead to certain accomplishments in rehearsal and performance and each tends to experience certain limitations.

Actors' strong suits and weaknesses

Each of these will bring definite strengths and some weaknesses to the rehearsal process. An actor who is a *high visual* will be very good in these categories:

- *Freedom from distractions.* They are able to shut out background noise and activity and stay highly focused on the task at hand.
- *Consistency, repetition.* They are able to set things, partly due to a love of precision, and have no difficulty doing something the same way it was done last time, a great boon once the director decides to set things.
- *Efficient execution of business.* They take in instructions carefully and precisely, do not in fact crave a lot of choice, so blocking and movement instructions will be followed to the letter.
- *Speeding up tempo.* Because they tend to speak quickly in any case, while other actors may end up indulging themselves in pauses, they will inevitably have no trouble keeping things moving.
- *Finding line rush clusters.* Their own thought processes tend to result in rushed statements with almost no space between words, so this effect in line reading is readily available.
- *Delivering throw-away lines.* Because their tempo inclinations do not allow room for a great deal of emphasis or stretching of words, they are very good at undercutting.

- *Communicating tension, trapped states.* They carry a certain amount of upper body tension, which in playing these emotions can be an actual boon, particularly where a comic effect, in which the character feels trapped, is desired.
- *Staring intently.* Others sometimes feel stared down by visuals, who do not blink or look away as often as others, as if their eye head-lights are on bright, so when this is needed, they are perfectly capable of providing it.
- *Focusing up and out.* While other actors feel compelled to connect with each other and are challenged by cheating forward, this is an easily accessed state for visuals.
- *Posture.* They tend to have a straight back so sitting and standing tall are no problem.
- *Stillness.* Visuals simply do not feel the need to move much, so will rarely have distracting, random movements.
- *Giving focus.* As noted above, intense watching is a natural inclination, which can transfer easily to allowing others to take stage.

I would say high visuals may excel in neurotic Woody Allen type comedies where characters are overwhelmed by their circumstances. They are also likely to be the most reliable and consistent over the course of a long run.

Conversely, they are likely to be stiff and unimaginative in terms of stage movement, will tend to rush everything, and can be vocally high, breathy and tedious.

A *high auditory* performer will be a delight to work with insofar as the following characteristics are involved.

- *Listening.* Simply engaging in the give and take of conversation gives them pleasure which translates well onstage.
- *Phrasing.* They are likely to come up with imaginative, compelling ways of clustering words and thoughts.
- *Coloring words.* They have an inherent inclination towards onomatopoeia, wherein words are not merely spoken but are shaped to sound like their meaning.
- *Sensuality of language.* The act of speaking is a sensual experience for auditories and that sense of pleasure and relish often come across strongly.

- *Non-verbal sounds.* Embellishing the script with sighs, groans, hums, sharp intakes of breath and other vocalized additions comes naturally to those who tend to add these in normal conversation.
- *Diction.* Sharp consonants, sometimes used as verbal weapons, are easily accessed by auditories.
- *Vocal pyrotechnics, contrasts.* They will not hesitate to find hills, valleys and explosions of sounds to add variety and surprise.
- *Self-talk.* While many actors find monologs where characters are talking to themselves awkward, high auditories often already embrace this kind of communication with self.
- *Coining.* Other actors may seem too slick and rehearsed, but this group will search and discover the words and phrases in a convincing impression of the first time.
- *Physical relaxation.* They are rarely tense or tight so will appear at ease onstage.
- *Finding an inner voice, interior monolog.* Just as they may actually talk out loud to themselves, they also will have no difficulty finding the internal self-talk in which their characters engage.

Über-auditories are likely to be particularly adept at classical works, especially Restoration or drawing-room comedies, where repartee or sharp dialogue exchange is crucial. In any play where characters have extended monologs with no implied movement, they are likely to make compelling, engaging and varied choices.

Alas, they may feel the need to take a lot of time to talk over any aspect of rehearsal. While far less stiff than visuals, they also will tend not to need to move much and therefore not contribute to the blocking of a scene. They may come up with a performance that is far more interesting to listen to than watch.

High kinos are often the most compelling actors to work with because they are so comfortable in their own bodies and in touch with their emotions. Their strengths include:

- *Willingness to jump in and try something, risk taking.* They are fundamentally brave and exploratory where others may be cautious and inhibited.
- *Self-staging, telling the story physically.* When they tell you about their day, kinos tend to get up on their feet and walk through the events, pantomiming responses, so they are naturally at ease when this is desirable within a performance.
- *Inventing business: both organic and random.* While many actors report "I just don't know what to do with my hands," this is never a problem for a high kino, who will easily find physical ways to connect with the context of the script and with tackling more abstract movement challenges.
- *Raising stakes, heightening emotion.* They can be dramatic (some would say over-reactors) in everyday life, but this has a big pay-off when playing in a large emotional space is required.
- *Reacting.* Specifically, they almost always show you the impact of what you have said to them, very useful in a large theatre where responses need to read to the back of the house. (It is not unusual for a high kino to respond to a devastating verbal put down as if it were a physical blow, reeling back, showing how much it hurt and all the effort it is taking to recover.)
- *Empathy.* Kinos will feel your pain or catch whatever is going on with the character, identifying and connecting deeply.
- *Shifting/changing emotion quickly.* This can translate to moodiness offstage, but the mercurial shifts made by characters are therefore no problem.
- *Finding animal, earthy, erotic impulses.* High kinos tend to be closer to animal and sensory based inclinations, which can add exciting, rooted dynamics to performance.
- *Freedom from self-consciousness.* Connected to the willingness to jump in and try things is the ability not to second guess or worry about embarrassing themselves that makes for open experimentation.
- *Physical contact with others.* They like to touch and be touched, may in fact crave contact, so this transfers effortlessly into ensemble and partner connections.

- *Believably playing the struggle in searching for and finding words*. While auditories may coin more smoothly, kinos know what it is like to be at a loss for words and can believably play that.
- *Sense of danger, unpredictability*. These are the actors most likely to surprise and to reveal characters flirting with violence and irrational behavior.

A high kino may be the most comfortable with film work, able to give something different on each take and free of the need for consistency, though their great love of the energy of a live audience may also make them do anything it takes to connect with that audience. They may then excel in deeply felt immediate moments, but also in contexts where the work needs to be big, personal and unabashedly emotional.

Unfortunately, they may have trouble setting or repeating anything the same way they did it last time, which can be frustrating when returning at the next rehearsal to work you had hoped was set. They may get bored and need frequent breaks. They may respond in an overly emotional way to rehearsal criticism and may take dangerous and sometimes inappropriate risks.

Back in Chapter 1, we discussed how a highly kinesthetic actor having trouble pronouncing a word may need to be guided to sense the difference between how he is saying the word now feels vs. how it actually feels to pronounce it correctly. An auditory actor will be the easiest to correct in this category because she will hear the wrong and right pronunciation immediately. A visual actor may need to be shown what the position of the lips, teeth and tongue look like in the initial pronunciation and then the correct one, possibly looking in a mirror and imitating the teacher/director through sight.

The protean actor will be one who can connect with performers of any modality and, more importantly, can shift, embrace, overlap and pull out the best of V, A and K in themselves to fulfill various performance requirements.

Directors' success secrets

Aside from interfacing with other actors, the performer's most crucial relationship is with her director. Actors and directors are bound, for good or bad, in a symbiotic relationship of great intensity, where trust is paramount. What they share and discover together in rehearsal provides the core of the performance and its level of effectiveness or the lack thereof. To this end, we will now explore director preferences, when they are strongly engaged in one of the modalities.

Here is a similar set of monologs, except we are now hearing from those in charge in terms of how they like to work. Again, while most directors cross modalities, it is useful to start with those who have an extreme commitment to V, A or K. Take the same approach, whether working alone or in a group, as in the former section in terms of speaking and bring this material to life. In class, give students preparation time and ask them to present the monologs in class and then respond to questions from the resident "studio audience."

Crucial questions

- What does a director do?
- What are the major problems or challenges?
- What do you most dislike in the work of other directors?

Visual

The way I see it a director paints pictures for the audience. It's my job to illuminate the text. I look closely at the script, hoping to glimpse the playwright's vision, which I then reveal to cast and designers. Each day we look for something to add and finally we unveil the work and help the audience see the big picture! That's the moment it all comes clear for me – and for them! In rehearsal and production meetings, I try to use colorful language and vivid images to show people what I mean. I always ask others what they are looking for. I also keep a close watch on everything I say and try to stay focused. I love it when I can get an actor or designer to see eye-to-eye with me. I can always see it has happened by the look on his face. What I hate most is a vague show with no focus, unclear ideas, limited scope and no overview! The real secret of directing? Clarity. If you observe every detail closely, you can shed light on any script. Oh, and never get so caught in your own vision that you forget things often look different from someone else's perspective. My best advice for every rehearsal? Keep your eyes open.

Auditory

My secret? Unlike some, I listen to my cast. I listen to my crew. I say to them, "You have a problem, you talk to me." I hate discord. I am sick to death of loud, thundering directors who sound off all the time! Oh sure, they get people to listen at first, but eventually everyone just tunes out. But I also *hate* actors who have nothing to say and give you the silent treatment when you ask to hear their ideas. Oh, and actors who mumble or, maybe worse yet, roar instead of speaking well. Puleeze. The big challenge of directing? First of all, figure out what the playwright is trying to say! What message does she want us to hear about our lives? At the end, what do we want our audiences to say to their friends about this show? When this team talks about the experience years from now, what will *we* say? Along the way, it's all about orchestrating the entire group, hearing any kind of dissonance and immediately seeking harmony. Hey, it's about fine-tuning! At staff meetings I try to deliver sound arguments without (and here I do not always succeed) talking too long. I have been told that I could sometimes say less. Whatever. My most valuable advice? Stay in tune with your staff. You can't plan everything. Sometimes you just have to play it by ear.

Kinesthetic

I hate a show that just sits there and I love a show that rocks! I try *hard* to avoid all the stumbling blocks to solid rehearsal communication. I tread lightly, stay sensitive, and keep everyone close. I keep my finger on the pulse of the whole show. You gotta know when to stroke, when to poke, how to hustle and how to nudge. Actors respond to your warmth or coolness, your roughness or your tenderness, your closeness or your distance. You've got to stay in touch with their feelings. Designers need to grasp that you are *there* for them and will carry them through it all – on your *back* if you have to! I try to never let anyone down. Oh, sure sometimes you meet with resistance. Sometimes you've got to kick some ass! Strong-arming can pull you through at those moments, but then you risk losing contact with the cast and staff which is, well, devastating. I hate feeling like the heavy! So I try … I … um … where was I? Oh, right! I try to stay open and caring. You know, a hug can help someone get back up when they are down. As long as we're all tight, we can iron out any problems that may come up on the way to opening night. That's when we all want to breathe deep and feel good!!

These monologs demonstrate high V, A or K patterns of expression. While many of us are more subtle blends, pure preference types are all around us. When I ask my students to identify directors within our department who are strongly engaged in each modality, they never have any trouble producing examples instantly. These extremes are the best places to start noticing.

If a director's rehearsal inclinations are unlike your own, I hope you now have sufficient awareness to recognize how you can respectfully interact, adjust, and get the most from the way that director functions, instead of feeling overwhelmed and defeated by your differences.

Sample VAK monologs from plays

Just as some people move actively between modalities and some stay largely in a favored mode, so do characters. In the following three monologs, notice how consistently the predicates of the speakers reveal the modes in which they are experiencing the world.

Visual (Steve from *Say Goodnight, Gracie* by Ralph Pape):

Now, you have to picture this: the rain, the two of us standing together on the sidewalk, not moving, just looking at each other, in close-up, the camera cutting back and forth between our faces.

And then she turned, and walked away. And as I watched her, I could see the camera pulling back for a long shot ... and I saw her about to become a memory and I remembered watching her walking with her friends, it was like a slow-motion flashback you know, in the rain, the wind blowing in her hair ... and I ran after her and I held her shoulders and ... I turned her around and I said to her: the very first time I saw you, you were walking in the rain, I saw you from a window and you looked harmless, and even though I didn't know who you were, I wanted to take off my coat and put it around you, which you would never have let me do, but I thought at that moment ... that it would have been possible not to be afraid of anything ... if only I could pretend that I could protect her.

I just want you to see it.

Auditory (Nicolas from *One for the Road* by Harold Pinter):

I'm talking about sexual intercourse ...

Does she ... fuck? Or does she ... ? Or does she ... like ... you know ... What does she like? I'm talking about your wife. Your *wife*. You heard the old joke? Does she fuck? Does she fuck! It's ambiguous, of course.

Do you know the man who runs this country? No? Well, he's a very nice chap. He took me aside the other day, last Wednesday, I think it was, he took me aside, at a reception, visiting dignitaries, he took *me* aside, *me*, and he said to me, he said, in what I can describe as a hoarse whisper, Nic, he said, Nic, that's my name, Nic, if you ever come across anyone whom you have a good reason to believe is getting on my tits, tell them one thing, tell them honesty is the best policy.

Kinesthetic (Pale from *Burn This* by Lanford Wilson):

> Goddamn this fuckin' place, how can anybody live in this shit city? I'm not doin' it, I'm not driving through this goddamn sewer, every fuckin' time. Who are these assholes? Some bug eyed, fat-lipped half nigger, all right; some of my best friends, thinks he owns this fuckin' *space*. The city's got this space specially reserved for his private use. Twenty-five fuckin' minutes I'm driving around this garbage street; I pull up this space, I look back, this fuckin' baby-shit green Trans Am's on my ass going *beep-beep*. I get out, this fucker says that's *my space*. I showed him the fuckin' tire iron; I told the fucker, you want this space, you're gonna wake up tomorrow, find you slept in your fuckin' car.
>
> I'm trying to parallel-park in the only fuckin' space in a twenty-block radius, you don't crawl up my butthole in your shit-green Trans Am and go *beep-beep*!

Read the monologs above silently. Then go back over the self-descriptions of Vs, As and Ks from the last chapter, this time recognizing every item on these lists as a potential detail of characterization. Using the checklists, layer in elements as you read the material out loud, segueing from simply recognizing elements of behavior to using them as building blocks to creating a performance.

Synesthesia

Synesthesia is a term used for switching or combining modalites. It comes from ancient Greek words for "together" and "sensation." In cases where shifts occur beyond the control of the individual it can be considered a neurological condition requiring treatment. However, if controlled, it can be considered a highly desirable NLP skill, assisting in communicating with others and in providing the performer with a fascinating variety of performance choices and the capacity to demonstrate versatility.

Plays rarely occur on ordinary days in the lives of characters. In fact, they often occur on the single most important and life-altering day. Because they are about major events, involving challenge, conflict and change, it is entirely possible for characters to shift, switch, blend and overlap modalities as they respond to various plot elements. Even a single monolog recounting a mega-event may involve the character switching and blending as the story progresses. Notice how the following character's verbs switch in a synesthetic way as he experiences his particular universe (Bickham from *Does a Tiger Wear a Necktie?* by Don Petersen).

I wasn't ashamed! I was *disgusted*!! I was sick to my stomach. He made me puke … just like *you* do. That lousy sonofabitch! I spent my life *thinkin'* of him … *lookin'* for him. I dreamed for years of how him and me would be together some day. Get together! That's *veerry* funny. Him and me get together.

We talked all right. He told me stories … dirty little barber stories. And out of a clear blue sky, he says, "You wanna see a picture of my wife and kid?" I think maybe … maybe he's talking about me and my mother, or somethin'. Maybe he's recognized me, for Chrissakes. He pulls out the picture, see, and brings it over and hands it to me. You wanna know what it was? You know what it was? A picture of some whorey lookin' blonde with her dress up to her ass and a baby sittin' on her lap. A baby … a baby boy. I don't know what's happenin'! I think it's gonna be a picture of *me* or something! I start shakin' all over. He's standin there grinnin' at me. He brings his hand down on my knee.

I drew a blank, see. I look at his face. I look at his grinning, slimy face. I pull the cloth off me and get up. He says, "Hey, I ain't through yet. What are ya doin'?" I *hit* him. I hit him *hard*. He don't know *nothin'*. He goes flat on his ass … his nose busts like a ketchup bottle! I'm standin' over him … him whimperin' and cryin'. I get down on top of him, and I *hit* him! I *hit* him and *hit* him! Him screamin' for the bulls, and me hittin' him.

Then, everything's quiet all of the sudden. I look down at him. I look down at the *barber* who's my father. He's bleeding like a stuck-pig. I look down at him ... and I know ... I know just what I've been waitin' for *all my life.*

Whaddya looking at? Whaddya looking at, *Doctor?* You like the story? You got what you wanted. You got me off stuff. You cured me, Doc, and now I belong to you.

Exploratory monologs

While it may be very clear when a character is in a V, A or K state, many scripts are sufficiently complex that only experimentation will reveal the most compelling combination of choices. Here are two speeches to help explore VAK. These are great, rich monologs in which characters describe events, images, words spoken and feelings which are very important to them.

> ALONE: Read through each speech just to get a sense of the words, ideas and feelings. then go back and attempt the speech in full visual mode. Do the same thing with auditory and kinesthetic. After working through both speeches ask yourself what clues seem strongest as to the character's preference and if there are times where the characters switches or blends modalities.

> GROUP: Work in groups of three. Each member draw V, A or K and develop the monolog between one meeting and the next. Present the monologs back to back. Discuss what elements of the monolog are brought out by each mode. Have the group provide feedback for actors on how to more fully realize the modality chosen, then go back and rehearse the material later for a second, more informed presentation.

Timmy from The Subject was Roses *by Frank Gilroy*

This character has recently been discharged from the army and returned home. He has spent some reunion weeks with his family but has decided it is now time to move out on his own, knowing full well his father will object and try to keep him home longer. There is an interesting tension in the speech because all the father's lines (though easy to imagine) have been cut to make it a monolog, so it is important to stop and listen and respond the father's interruptions. The relationship with an imaginary but fully present listener is a great acting challenge. This encounter usually takes place in the family kitchen, so an upstage entrance, and a kitchen table and chairs are useful for staging the event.

TIMMY:

Good morning, Pop. Mom said you wanted to see me.
    Well, yeah, I am leaving.
    No, I don't mind telling you why. I just think it's best. For everyone.
    No, that's not why I'm going. It's not about last night
    Pop.
    Pop! I'm not leaving because of anything that happened last night … I always intended to leave. I planned to stay a couple of weeks and then go.
    Pop?
    Pop!
    Listen to me!!
    There was a dream I used to have about you and me … It was always the same … I'd be told that you were dead and I'd run crying into the street … Someone would stop me and ask why I was crying and I'd say, "My father's dead and he never said he loved me." I had that dream again last night. But this morning something occurred to me that I'd never thought of before. It's true you've never said you love me. But it's also true that I've never said those words to you.
    I say them now. I love you, Pop.
    I love you.

Suzanne from Picasso at the Lapin Agile *by Steve Martin*

This is a very different monolog in that the character is describing an event from the past and her listener could be any number of people. In the play itself, she is speaking to a group of fellow patrons in a bistro. But in adapting it for solo performance, it could be delivered to the character's therapist, a group of girl-friends hanging out, or to an encounter or recovery group of some kind, among other possible choices. It is important as you speak the lines to go back and relive the memory so fully that the listener can experience it almost firsthand.

> I ... It was about two weeks ago. I was walking down the street one afternoon and I turned up the stairs into my flat and I looked back and he was there framed in the doorway, looking up at me. I couldn't see his face, because the light came in from behind him and he was in shadow and he said, "I am Picasso." And I said, "Well, so what?" And then he said he wasn't sure yet, but he thinks that it means something in the future to be Picasso. He said that occasionally there is a Picasso, and he happens to be him. He said the twentieth century has to start somewhere and why not now. Then he said, "May I approach you," and I said, "Okay." He walked upstairs and picked up my wrist and turned it over and took his fingernail and scratched deeply on the back of my hand. In a second, in red, the image of a dove appeared. Then I thought, "Why is it that someone who wants me can hang around for months, and I even like him, but I'm not going to sleep with him; but someone else says the right thing and I'm on my back, not knowing what hit me?"
>
> So the next thing I know he's inside the apartment and I said, "What do you want?" and he said he wanted my hair, he wanted my neck, my knees, my feet. He wanted his eyes on my eyes, his chest on my chest. He wanted the chairs in the room, the notepaper on the table; he wanted the paint from the walls. He wanted to consume me until there was nothing left. He said he wanted deliverance, and that I would be his savior. And he was speaking Spanish, which didn't hurt, I'll tell you. Well at that point, the word *no* became like a Polish village: unpronounceable. (*Proudly*) I held out for seconds!
>
> Frankly, I didn't enjoy it that much 'cause it was kinda quick.

ALONE: How does reading the monolog V, A, K or syno make you respond? What insights do you get from each trip through the speech? Which verbs jump out and which images prevail? What do you know about this character as a result of taking him or her in three different directions?

GROUP: Discuss what elements are brought out by each modality. Critique each performer in terms of what elements are right on the money and what the actor could do to be "even better" in terms of mastering V, A, K or S for a blended interpretation.

If you are in an acting class, each performer should go back again and work on refining the monolog based on the feedback received and your own needs as a performer. Do you want to master the mode you originally drew? Do you want to explore switching within the speech and determine where the character might change modes because of something that happens? Determine what NLP-based work will help you grow the most. When the material is presented for the second time in class, focus on the ways it has grown deeper and richer because of NLP, and how the actor might continue to develop the speech.

Original monolog – "The Best Day of My Life"

Experiencing all three modalities in a very short period of time is not unusual. This exercise gives you a creative way of using the language and transitioning swiftly. Write a monolog in which the character moves in some way between V, A and K. Then practice performing in such a way that allows you to switch on a dime. The story may be entirely true, entirely fictional or a blend of actual events, enhanced by artistic license.

Here are two examples:

"The Hospital, or The Best Day of My Life" by Jackie Peterman Wolfer

Checking in was nothing like checking out. Going in everything seemed darker, narrower, sketchier, out of focus.

Looking back I can remember watching the nurse talk with my parents, and I can see myself sitting in the corner. So still. I wanted my posture more than anything to show how upset I was with my new surroundings. I looked down into the clear, clean white tiled floor, and starting back at me is the reflection of a girl. A pale, starved, unhealthy, sad girl. I looked up to find my parents towering over me. My mother is crying and extending her arms to me, like I'm supposed to hug her? I look up at my dad, and it's the same thing that I've seen for the last twenty years of my life. Absolutely nothing. I try my hardest to avoid eye contact with them. I want them to see how angry I am at them. How can these people love me so much and leave me in a place like this? The nurse grabs my arms and leads me away without any good-byes. I can remember looking down at her hand wrapped around my arm. Her hand looked so big around my little arm. It was at that moment I knew how sick I was.

On the other side of the doors I hear the horrifying sound of a woman wailing and crying like she's having a break-down. I stop and realize it's my mother, and I quickly close my eyes and try to drown out the noise. Suddenly there is silence, and the only sound is that of my heels clicking with the cold hard floor. As we walk the line to my room, we pass doors on both sides of me. If I concentrate hard enough I can hear the sounds of them being slammed in my face, of the keys turning in their locks. If I listen even closer, I can hear the sounds of the girls inside crying, whispering, moaning. I can almost hear them shivering. For the next three weeks I became those sounds behind a faceless door.

But then ... something happened! ... and I don't know where or when or how it happened, but something clicked inside of me. I felt alive again. Suddenly like a ton of bricks it hit me that I may actually be okay! Three years of my life wasted, and go figure I may actually be okay! Suddenly I found myself at those doors that I had passed through three weeks earlier and my excitement suddenly turned to anxiety. I felt like I was twelve years old again at one of my soccer games. I began to wonder if anyone would be waiting for me on the other side. I mean people had always told me "this is your last straw", but did they mean it this time? I mean my boyfriend and friends had already abandoned me ... what would make my parents any different ... right? Well, my fears were put to rest as soon as I saw my mother standing there crying and smiling. This time I smiled and ran to her and hugged her, and kissed her and loved her like I had never hugged or kissed or loved anyone before. I was over-whelmed with joy. Then I felt the graze of my dad's hand on my shoulder and I look over and my heart stops. This is not the same thick-skinned man I had left behind. This man was crying. I had never seen this man cry before. He grabbed me and hugged me so tight I could barely breathe, but it didn't matter. I had been waiting for that hug for twenty fucking long years and it felt great. I had never felt so loved or like I had so much love to give. It was the start of a new beginning for all of us. It was the best day EVER!

In the speech above, the sequence is clear. In the one below, the speaker more rapidly shifts through the various modalities before a kinesthetic finale.

"Poetry Explosion, or The Best Day of My Life" by Sarah Wells

When I go to poetry readings, I fall in love with a different person every ten minutes. I think it has to do with the immediate emotional availability. These people I've never seen before are suddenly blind to society's rules of staying pleasant and polite. All of a sudden it's OK to talk about love and death and bowel movements and war. It's OK to yell and cry and swoon. It's captivating. Sometimes I'm not even listening to the poem. I sit there, mesmerized by the poets who have stepped on to the stage to reveal themselves to the audience. I watch the women curve their hips to their personal anthems and close their eyes to give more life to their syllables. The skinny indie boys flap their arms to the beat of the words and perspiration starts to shimmer on their foreheads. Crumpled papers are thrown to the ground as these wordsmiths carve out new meaning in their perform-ance. These poems flow out of them. It's like their souls are singing. I sit there, awestruck and envious, quiet and self-conscious, and I want so desperately to expose myself like that. I want to vomit up passion onstage and let myself feel the words rocketing out of me. I want other people to ride the rhythm of my emotions and wrap their minds around my feelings. I want to curve my hips to my personal anthem and move my arms to my self-constructed cadence. I want the audience to fall in love with me.

This original monolog assignment can provide you with a rich and juicy audition speech. Aside from the confidence of knowing that no one else will be presenting this material, the fact that the character moves between modalities as the story progresses forces a compelling dynamic and a real sense of change and development in the character. The "Best Day" format lends itself to a satisfying conclusion with a sense of celebration. However, you could pick any crucial, life-changing day as a starting point.

In the exercises in this and the previous chapter, the experi-ence of VAK has been explored from a variety of perspec-tives. Each mode has been entered (and exited) through various doors. Through both scripted and improvised exercises, we have experienced:

- speaking the tendencies and modeling the behavior of each mode,
- switching quickly between modes,
- gaining comfort through game playing, storytelling and hypothetical discussions,
- recognizing language signals and habits through varying speeches on the same topic
- examining and inhabiting the same sets of words and the same characters, loaded three very different ways, for an understanding of how people can vary.

Summary

The mastery of VAK can be achieved by experiencing the self-descriptions of actors with a strong preference for each. Rather than there being a preferred mode of performance, an actor who engages each one will offer specific strengths and weaknesses to the rehearsal and performance process. Because of their intimate engagement with directors, it is helpful for actors to also study those with high V, A or K tendencies who may be guiding them in developing characterization. In examining playscripts, it is often clear exactly where a character is located by his choice of predicates, which may be squarely lodged in a single modality or synesthetically switching. The capacity to master synesthesia can serve both rehearsal interaction and actor versatility. Further mastery can come from exploring monologs of complexity and ambiguity for the most compelling available choices and by writing and performing original monologs in which characters progress through all three modes.

Words/ideas to remember

modality performance strengths and weaknesses
synesthesia
VAK actor preferences
VAK director preferences

4

REFRAMING

There is nothing either good or bad, but thinking makes it so.
William Shakespeare

Imagine a favorite painting or photograph. If it is one that hangs in a familiar spot, envision the way it is now framed. Now take this same picture, and in your imagination, place it in each of the following:

- a wooden oak frame
- a shiny chrome frame
- a gilded baroque frame with golden grape clusters
- matted and placed in a large sleek, black plastic frame
- placed behind a piece of clear acrylic
- held up by four thumbtacks, one at each corner.

What surrounds or does not surround the picture, changes the impression it makes so much as to transform the picture itself, sometimes almost beyond recognition. Reframing a picture can bring new and vibrant life to it. NLP is about reframing experience and perception.

Here is how a friend of mine, in a few words, reframed my understanding of an entire relationship. I was complaining to this friend about how little I (an engagingly lively artiste of the theatre) had in common with my father (a static, deadly engineer/ scientist), who in his spare time would buy old broken clocks at flea markets, take them apart and lay out all the parts on his work-bench, then meticulously put them all back together so that they worked. I was commenting on how bizarre and incomprehensible all this was and my friend said "Well, you do that."

What?

"You break down all the components of acting to their smallest parts and then put them back together so it becomes clear how they work. That's why your books do well."

Well.

That gave me pause. In one simple statement, she took me from feeling disconnected to recognizing a kinship I had never even considered. And filled me with gratitude.

NLP is basically a limitless set of reframes, ways to take an aspect of your life and place it in another frame or free it from a frame so that it works better for you. Some of us believe the founders of NLP should have called it Reframes, a more accessible and easily comprehensible title.

Throughout this book we have been reframing perception. Some examples:

- how language can capture and alter experience
- how an apology can be vastly improved
- how we progress through levels of competence
- how self-study can open up insight and growth
- how we can anchor our resource states for ready availability
- how modalities frame the particular world one experiences
- how tolerance and empathy can grow out of entering other modalities
- how predicates and eye-accessing cues reveal filters
- how submodalities add richness and complexity to experience
- how shifting these submodalities can place positive and negative memories where they will serve us best
- how VAK can lead to understanding those we might have formerly found completely mystifying
- how scripts can be perceived and explored in new and engaging ways
- how synesthesia can be a source of power and versatility.

VAK can reframe relationships to work successfully. Two kinds of actors who tend to experience the greatest tension are high kinos and high visuals. Think about it. Someone who needs a lot of space and craves contact vs. someone who needs little and does not necessarily like to be touched. Someone who goes balls out vs. someone contained. Someone loose vs. someone tight. Someone who needs to do it vs. someone who just needs to see it. The tendencies of these two modalities are often in opposition. If you are a high visual, you might have been driven crazy by your kino scene partner before you understood that his actions were not designed to irritate you but were based on his filter of the world and his needs for ways to express himself. If you had a photo of him, the frame of the image you carried in your head before might have had a sign "JERK" at the bottom. After some VAK education, you might re-label that photo "MY CRAZY, LOVEABLE KINO FRIEND."

Ironically, this visual–kino tension has provided the fodder for countless love stories that start with the uptight visual or someone who behaves with those classic characteristics (Hepburn and countless others) encountering the wild, irreverent kino (Tracy, Bogie, et al.), first with major conflict, then learning to appreciate and even ultimately adore the other. At the fade-out, they have reframed their perceptions of each other, she has given him class, he has given her guts, and all is well.

Jokes are reframes, because you believe you are headed in one direction or context and then the punch line puts you in another. Events are set up in one frame, which is quickly and drastically changed. Two examples:

What happened to the lovers who mixed up their jar of lubricant with their jar of window putty?

Their window fell out.

What happened when the Pope went to Mount Olive?

Popeye hit him.

71

In the first instance, we are fully expecting a punch line with a sexual context and we get something else altogether. In the second we expect something else all together and get a punch-line related to sex.

"Frame" indicates the assumptions that shape and surround how we perceive something and the choices we think we have. We all know and use the phrase "frame of mind." NLP offers frames of reality.

Transformative vocabulary

Nowhere is the linguistic component of NLP more vividly demonstrated than in this category, which demonstrates that while language is not experience, it certainly can create experience. The choice of one single word over another can reframe perception so that it is transformed. Go through the list below, imagining a circumstance for each word in the left column. Then re-imagine that circumstance if you made the decision to describe it instead with the word on the right. This is not going to be appropriate all the time because sometimes the word on the left accurately describes how you feel, and with good reason, and softening or modifying the experience will not be the honest path. But there are countless other instances where, in order to deal with an issue more successfully and get on with your life, the reframe on the right will be tremendously helpful.

OK or NOT	*OFTEN BETTER*
angry	disenchanted
afraid	uncomfortable
anxious	expectant
confused	curious
disappointed	delayed
exhausted	recharging
failed	stumbled
frustrated	challenged
impatient	anticipating
irritated	stimulated

OK or NOT	*OFTEN BETTER*
overloaded	stretching
overwhelmed	challenged
rejected	deflected
excluded	misunderstood
lazy	storing energy
stupid	unresourceful
bored	searching

Or consider these pairs:

GOOD	*BETTER*
awake	energized
curious	fascinated
lucky	blessed
interested	enthralled
enjoy	relish
calm	serene

NLP warm-ups

Traditional acting warm-ups most often have a major kinesthetic component, which may involve stretching, shaking, breathing, alignment and aerobic components, as if the intention is to bring the actor's body more alive and ready for subsequent activity. If a vocal warm-up is added, it may involve tensing and releasing, respirating, rooting sound, shaping sound, and precision drills, getting the actor ready to explore and express auditorily. Sometimes a guided meditation is added in which actors visualize themselves in another setting and/or in a more tranquil state. So warm-ups often stimulate the VAK senses.

Because there are so many of the above warm-ups available in other sources, we will concentrate here on some specifically tied to NLP perspectives and processes. The activity practiced by many that most directly intersects with NLP is meditation.

An important reframe most of us need is to stop believing that everything can be solved by our working it out consciously, logically, step by step. NLP work is often about shutting off the conscious mind and turning things over to the unconscious.

Warm-ups tend to focus on producing a meditative state. While meditation is largely associated with Eastern cultures, its value in stress reduction and healing has been established through Western scientific research. All the activities below should last 10 to 20 minutes. All may be (though it is not essential) accompanied with music playing quietly the background. New age, chants and gentle classical music work best. Nothing with lyrics unless it is a phrase repeated so frequently that you can let it disappear from your consciousness.

Meditation

1   Find a spot where you can be completely comfortable in a sitting position.
2   If there is a particular problem or issue you have been working on, identify it, but then let it fade from your consciousness.
3   Select a mantra to repeat over and over. It may be simply some sounds, such as the classic "om." It may be a phrase you like such as "smooth and silken," or a state you would like to achieve, such as "peace and tranquility" or "calm and cool." A classic traditional Hindu mantra, considered one of the most powerful in existence, is "Om namah shivaya" (pronounced "ohm nah ma shee vie'ah") which translates literally as "I bow to Shiva" or, more meaningfully, what the god Shiva influences in us. So it ultimately means bowing "to the supreme reality, the true inner self, the consciousness that dwells in all of us." A more rough but effective translation would be "Let what should be for me, be."
4   Close your eyes. Take five deep diaphragmatic breaths, then allow your breath to grow more and more shallow throughout the process.
5   Begin repeating the mantra out loud, then sotto voce, then just in your head. This will occupy and distract your conscious mind. Because it is hard for many of us to shut off conscious thinking, this distraction is essential, while freeing your unconscious to take over.
6   After the period of time you have allotted, let your breathing return to normal, slowly bring back into consciousness your

awareness of your surroundings, open your eyes and proceed with the activities of the day.

VAK meditation

If you have a tendency for your conscious mind to still wander or invade during the process of meditation, engage it further when you are repeating your mantra by:

1   imagining it being written across the screen of your mind, seeing it in various fonts, letting the letters change colors, letting the word or phrase drift toward you, away, up or down, and/or letting it increase or decrease in size;
2   imagining it spoken by famous performers (James Earl Jones? Judi Dench? Sean Connery?) whose voices you admire, by people in your life of whom you are very fond, by chanting monks, a children's choir, any other diverting vocal group;
3   imagining, if there is not already background music, a sound-track in your mind, perhaps chimes or percussion accompanying the repetitions;
4   imagining a slight change in temperature, perhaps a gentle, soothing breeze;
5   imagine that you are floating lightly, freed from the confines of gravity;
6   imagine any physical sensation that you find soothing and enjoyable.

From the menu of choices above, experiment with which ones you enjoy the most and which compel and engage your pesky conscious mind for the duration of your meditation.

Mind Juggling

Ed Zwick came up with the idea for this exercise, based on brain hemisphere research, that perhaps the linear logical side of the brain and the freewheeling creative side could be brought into alignment through physical activity that would send energy back and forth between one's left and right sides. Acting requires connection and interaction between both hemispheres and so can benefit particularly from this alignment.

1   Take a juggling ball, bean bag or some other small object. If possible have a metronome set to beat each second or stand near a clock so you are aware of it ticking and can let that rhythm guide your activity.
2   Stand and let the ball move back and forth from one hand to the other at each ticking sound. Let your body tell you if you wish to dip slightly from side to side, toss the ball in the air, just hand it off, or whatever exchange mode helps you to comfortably settle into the rhythm.
3   Close your eyes and enjoy sending the energy back and forth between both sides of your body and brain, bringing them into a state of accord.
4   Add a mantra if you wish, with the repetition accompanying the passing of the object.
5   Savor the physical pleasure of the back and forth motion along with the sensation of welcoming your brain hemispheres into a state of alignment.

Partner breathing

This is an effective way to get on the same wavelength with someone who is a scene partner or with whom you will undertake some activity. It literally gets you breathing as one.

1   One of you sits on a chair, the other stands directly behind with hands placed on your partner's shoulders. Both close your eyes.
2   The seated partner should breathe deeply for a while so her breath pattern is clear and easy to connect with. The standing partner, once sensing that pattern, should join it.
3   Let breathing for both of you gradually settle into a more normal range.
4   Stay in this position for 5 minutes, then switch positions and repeat the entire process.

Core states

Connirae and Tamora Andreas, when doing research for their book on NLP and spirituality, *Core Transformation*, consulted with psychiatrists and other counselors, about what tends to be missing from someone's life when that person feels the need to get professional help. They found it was one or more of the following states:

1 Being

- Feeling fully present from inside out
- Totally involved and whole
- In the moment, undistracted
- Enjoying a sense of ongoing well-being

2 Okay-ness

- Experiencing deep, intrinsic worthiness
- Knowing you are all right just as you are
- Accepting, welcoming and even loving your limitations
- Feeling beyond judgment and righteousness

3 Inner peace

- Feeling a sense of calm
- Knowing a vibrant, harmonious *stillness*
- Allowing your inner mind to turn loose, discerning clarity within
- Letting things roll off your back

4 Lovingness

- Feeling reverence and respect for every person
- Approaching everyone with unconditional positive regard
- Responding with kindness and empathy
- Feeling as if you are a source of tenderness and warmth

5 Oneness

- Dissolving personal boundaries, sensing we are all one
- Enjoying absolute unity with all of life

- Feeling far more aware of what connects us all than of what separates us
- Able to surrender to something larger than yourself.

While the Andreas sisters did not present the core states in this order, I found that for myself this particular sequence is essential. If I am not being fully present, I am not likely to feel okay about myself. If I am not okay, I will not achieve a sense of peace. These first three are all about the individual and seem to me to need to be in place before I can reach out and connect with others. That being the case, a spirit of lovingness is the way to do so and that may then lead to the final core state, a sense of connectedness or oneness.

If these states are missing in our lives, leading to a sense of unbalance and ultimately a need to seek professional counseling, what if we simply made ourselves more available to them on a day to day basis? Would this not increase the likelihood of being in them powerfully on a more regular basis?

1   Take any of the meditative activities above, but before settling into a mantra, beckon the core states by willing yourself to be open and engaged in them.
2   One by one, make a commitment statement such as "For the next few hours I will achieve beingness, staying fully present and engaged in the here and now."
3   Move through a beckoning of each core state and a willingness to be open and embracing of each.
4   Then take your willingness and turn it over to your unconscious mind and transfer your consciousness to the repeating of a mantra.

VAK conjuring

Most of us tend to lag behind in at least one of the modalities, so it can be helpful to beckon and sharpen responses. While sitting quietly:

1   Visualize your favorite person in the world in a specific setting, your favorite animal, still life or other painting,

panoramic scenic viewpoint, colors drifting and changing, much beloved objects, films you particularly enjoy, things you like to see, give yourself a feast of visual sensations.

2   Hear the sound of your favorite musical instrument, sounds of nature, phrase or words of wisdom, the best compliment you have ever received as it was spoken, voices of your family members and loved ones, delightful laughter, your favorite song.

3   Conjure your favorite scents, including colognes, smells of nature, spices, any olfactory sensations that please you, imagine yourself in your favorite spot in which to be alone and contemplate, the feel of your most comfortable clothing against your skin, an emotional memory that you cherish, sensations of contact, such as holding hands and being hugged, recall the taste of favorite foods and flavors.

Use these VAK beckonings one after the other if you wish to awaken a synesthetic sense of flowing easily between modalities. Isolate one set as a way of preparing to experiment in a single modality either in improvisation or with scripted work.

Trunk packing

The above exercises can all be done alone or in the company of a group, but isolated in your own space. What follows is a group activity, an ice-breaker, a way to learn names of participants, and a pleasant refresher when something fun and sort of silly seems appropriate.

1   Place a large open box or upside-down wastebasket in the center of the room; this will be the trunk to be packed for the group's NLP journey.

2   Everyone select something imaginary to pack, that either starts with the first letter of your name and/or rhymes with it. Your choices do not have to make any actual sense or have any practical use on a journey, but if they reflect you, your tastes, or personal tendencies, that adds to the experience.

I might pack "Robert's roses," "Robert's robots," "Bob's books" or "Bob's knobs."

3   Gather in a standing circle. The first person says "On this trip, we are going to take ..." then completes the sentence while pantomiming carrying the objects to the box and placing them inside. If I am packing "Bob's books," I start holding a pile of them and carefully transport them and pack them in the "trunk."

4   The next person repeats the sentence and action exactly, before starting her own sentence and action.

5   Everyone goes through the process with the last person (the one standing on the other side of the first participant) re-packing for everyone in the group before finally putting in their own contribution.

(If there is a good-sized group and actors are struggling toward the end, give them lots of hints, side coaching and encouragement.)

Most groups have no trouble learning the names of everyone present in a very short period of time because of the strong associations and input from all three modalities. V, A and K are all loaded into the senses as you watch the action, while hearing the alliterative and/or rhymed phrase, while sensing what it will feel like to complete the action, and then you yourself repeat the sounds and complete the kinesthetic task, while seeing what you have just packed, so you have experienced each modality twice.

(NOTE: VAK loading can help you memorize anything more quickly. If you are having trouble remembering any kind of information, it may be that you have left out a V, an A or a K component in trying to load it into your memory. See memorization strategies in Chapter 6.)

Metaprograms

NLP provides what is for most of us a whole new way to frame our perception of how we tend to function in various circumstances. Until I encountered the list below, I thought I knew myself and my tendencies quite well, but then I realized that I had simply never examined myself in terms of these polarities.

Proactive/reactive

Do you readily take the initiative and make things happen or do you wait until prodded in some way by others? Do you have a tendency toward one or the other? If you sometimes do each, under what specific circumstances? Actors need to be proactive regarding their careers in one of the world's most competitive professions, but then they need to be reactive to requests from directors and other members of the production team.

Towards/away

Do you motivate yourself by setting a goal and heading toward it or by avoiding failure and humiliation? These can actually be equally motivating, but clearly the first is more enjoyable. You want to give a great performance, while avoiding being slammed by the critics.

In athletics competitions we often sadly see someone shift from one to the other. A young figure or speed skater making a first appearance at the Olympics will radiate sheer joy in being present and a "towards" motive to be placed, possibly even to secure a spot, any spot, on the podium. However, often the more experienced reigning gold-medal holder now finds himself trying to avoid losing the title, keeping "away" from defeat. And frequently a grim determination has replaced the sheer joy of being among the elite of the sport.

Internal/external

Do you tend to look to your own inner wisdom to determine your level of accomplishment, truly being true to yourself? Or do you tend to rely on the judgment of others, seeking approval and status, not sure how you did until all the votes are in?

Acting is a profession where we are constantly being judged, guided, given notes, feedback, blocking, instructions, yet which requires a secure inner belief in self to keep going in the face of rejection. It also requires the capacity to shift through what can sometimes be contradictory suggestions to find what works best

81

for you. Are you devastated by negative reviews or able to shake them off and move on?

Options/procedures

Do you like to have lots of choices on the job, in rehearsal, as part of any endeavor? Or do you like everything laid out, clear rules and guidelines so that you can feel secure and on track? High kinos tend to prefer the former and high visuals the latter.

Or do you like much freedom in some endeavors and to just be told exactly what to do in others?

General/specific

Are you a big-picture person, able to come up with great sweeping ideas and plans, and perhaps less effective at the details of execution? Or do you depend on others for the grand vision, but are highly adept at getting the work started, knowing exactly what has to be done first and developing an effective, detailed game plan? There are those who can come up with a brilliant overall production concept or scheme for fund-raising or increasing season subscription sales, but not the step-by-step process for achieving these; they may have no clue as to where to begin. That requires detail people, who know what the very first steps need to be and how to work in increments towards achievement.

Match/mismatch

Do you tend to find connections, see similarities, parallels and see ways in which elements match? Or are you better at determining what is wrong, not working and needs correction? I am an extreme matching person. Some of my books end with the phrase "Onstage and Off," and I constantly tend to notice how similar stage/screen acting is to acting our lives effectively. I intensely studied NLP and was possessed by how much it is like acting, even being motivated to write a book about it! But in this world of book writing, I also work regularly with copy editors (and would be a terrible one myself) who have to have mismatch radar, finding spelling, grammar, syntax, description problems and suggesting ways to fix them. They have to be very good at finding what is wrong.

Metaprograms self-analysis

(The form for this project is Appendix B.)

Ask yourself, in what context in both your life in and outside of the theatre are you likely to be or employ:

1 PROACTIVE – REACTIVE
2 TOWARDS – AWAY
3 INTERNAL – EXTERNAL
4 OPTIONS – PROCEDURES
5 GENERAL – SPECIFIC
6 MATCH – MISMATCH

In each pair, what are the choices you are more likely to make in most contexts?

From the entire list, what is the one choice you are least likely to make ever?

For most of us just starting to recognize that we *have* metaprograms reframes our perception of ourselves and can give us motive for changing some of them. It also reframes our view of friends we may have had trouble understanding before or persons with whom we seem to butt heads, never realizing that our metaprogram tendencies were in opposition. Aside from the insights we gain about self and colleagues, this also offers a new way of analyzing a character and her behavior, and can provide considerable insight into ways to play a role.

Metalanguage

Most of us have a tendency at least occasionally to make sweeping generalizations or to presume without evidence to know what others are thinking and feeling. The meta-model provides tools for reframing this awkward and usually entirely inaccurate choice of words into clarity. It is a set of linguistic tools that help crack the code (language) to get to the importance or richness of the experience (meaning) that words represent.

Patterns

1   *Unspecified nouns* and *pronouns*. Sample statement: "They did everything wrong here."

    Recommended response: Ask who, what, which, specifically?

2   *Unspecified verbs*. Sample statement: "She really hurt me." Note that it is not clear if a physical blow was struck or feelings were hurt.

    Response: Ask how, specifically, were you hurt?

3   *Nominalizations*. Using process words, usually verbs, that have been converted into nouns. For example "relationship" or "attention." The test is whether or not something can fit in a wheelbarrow and both these clearly cannot. Sample statements: "Our relationship sucks." "I need your attention."

    Response: Ask questions to get the word back from a noun to a verb. "How are you relating to each other now? How would you rather relate to him?" "You want attention? Tell me how I'm not attending you and how you would like me to."

4   *Polarity words*. Using words that absolutely limit the possibility of choice or exceptions: all, none, everybody, nobody, always, never. Sample statement: "He never, ever notices me."

    Response: Repeat "Never? Not even once? Has there ever been a time when he did? What was that like?"

5   *Mind reading*. Assuming you know what someone else thinks or what is going on with them. Or expecting them to know what you think or what is going on with you. Sample statements: "They all envied me." "They were going to fire me."

    Response : Ask "How specifically do you know that? What did they do or say that led you to that conclusion."

Other deletions and generalizations are below. Test yourself by imagining a friend has just made one of these statements and attempt to respectfully point out the information that is missing or the flaw in the reasoning: *Comparison*: "Bob's the best!" "I handled the audition very badly." *Judgment*: "I'm bad!" "She was obviously precast." *No possibility*: "I can't cry onstage." "I can't discipline myself." "Journals don't work for me." *Complete necessity*: "I have to warm up for at least three hours." *Complex equivalence*: "If you don't look at me when I'm talking to you, you're not paying attention." *Faulty presupposition*: "Since it's wrong to have sex with someone of the same sex, you two sinned." "What outfit are you wearing to the party?" *Cause and effect*: "He makes me mad." "She intimidates me."

Cautionary note: When you are trying to help someone clarify metalanguage or correct their metalanguage violations, be at your most pleasant, gentle in manner and respectful. And take your time. There should be no "Ah ha! I gottcha!" jumping on the other person's error. Do not be a Meta Monster!

Do you recognize yourself in any of the metalanguage patterns above? Do you recognize others in your life? Usually it is much easier with others than ourselves, so try this exercise. Which of these statements have you made recently?

I always …
I must …
I should …
I never …
I ought to …
I have to …

Go back over the list and for each statement ask yourself:

What would happen if I didn't?
When did I decide that?
Is this statement true and helpful for me right now?

Create a revise list that replaces words above with "I choose to …"

Once we sense and acknowledge these tendencies, we can consciously clarify our own statements and avoid confusing or misleading others. We can also more effectively advise others by more quickly determining what is *really* going on. And the patterns used by characters in a script can reveal much about how they confront, avoid or obfuscate experiences, information which can offer tremendous guidance in playing the role.

Rapport

Many of us believe, inaccurately, that rapport is accidental. We just have it with some people and not with others. But it can actually be cultivated, using the same tools we actors employ to build a characterization. The list below is often used in acting classes for each performer to analyze their own tendencies. Courses that employ imitation assignments ask students to capture the physical and vocal lives of their classmates through systematic analysis and practice. In playing a role, we identify which of our own characteristics are appropriate to the character and which need to be altered to meet the demands of playing her. In spite of being familiar with the actual categories, actors, in their offstage and rehearsal communication, sometimes flagrantly forget that these same elements are needed to get on someone else's wavelength. If you always speak louder than the other person while they respond sotto voce or if you gesture wildly when they are extremely contained, it is unlikely they will feel connected with and open towards you.

At the other extreme, some actors mirror and match others so completely that they sometimes seem to be mimicking them in a patronizing or mocking way, going through chameleon changes so rapidly that they seem to have lost any true sense of themselves, which can be equally off-putting. Rapport is a dance. It involves being sensitive and respectful of shifts on the part of your partners without actually *impersonating* them. In each category it is useful to ask how effective you are at calibrating. Most of us will be very skilled at some elements on the list and clueless in others, which need development. Then just start practicing dancing, with the goal of mastering all the categories.

Rapport checklist

Body

- Posture
- Leaning
- Crossing
- Filling space
- Head movement
- Facial expressions
- Eye movements
- Gestural patterns.

Sample suggestions for the rapport dance

If the other person is leaning against a wall or far back in their chair, you don't need to do exactly that, but be sure your posture is relaxed, loose and clearly not formal. You might support yourself with your hand on the seat or back of your chair as a complementary counterpoint to the other person's lean.

Voice

- Pitch
- Volume
- Tone
- Pronunciation
- Articulation
- Non-verbal sounds.

Sample suggestions for the rapport dance

In this case, it may be more like singing in harmony, avoiding the boring sameness of singing the same tune and offering complementary enhancement. Be particularly conscious of avoiding precise mimicry in all the above categories. If the other person is using an extremely high pitch, for example, just lighten up your own a bit, editing some of the deep bass notes. If the other person is mumbling or slurring, just be sure to back off on super-precise, clipped speech.

Language

- Word choice
- Syntax
- Predicates.

Sample suggestions for the rapport dance

If your partner is using lots of slang and casual language, you do not have to do the same, but definitely avoid formal word choices, be relaxed in vocabulary and use similar verbs and descriptions.

Most important

- Tempo/rhythm
- Breathing.

Sample suggestions for the rapport dance

These last two elements are crucial. If your timing is off – say you are still talking faster and placing heavier emphasis on words than your partner – it can undermine everything else you have accomplished. And breathing patterns, the depth and frequency of inhalation and exhalation, are key to timing. It is particularly important to stop and allow your partner time to breathe when she is contemplating or considering something, with respectful silence.

Breaking rapport

As desirable as it is to master, rapport can sometimes be a trap. I have a friend I tease about being a "rapport whore." You probably know some people like this as well. They fall instantly so in tune with anyone who enters their lives that they are constantly being hit on by creeps, unable to get away, trapped by chatterbox acquaintances or perfect strangers out in the world, unable to refuse to be interrupted when they have crucial work to do, and just plain stuck in encounters they do not wish to have. So it is as important to know when to cut off this dance as it is how to dance it.

Practice breaking off rapport as well, so you are able to escape when you need to. In fact, a good way to master the items on the list above is to identify (at least in your head) what it would be like to be totally out of sync with the person you are encountering before moving in the opposite direction in order to join them.

It is useful to identify when a character you are playing is in and out of rapport, or in which elements the character is skilled and where he is inept. Characters are often out of rapport because the nature of drama is conflict, but this makes it all the more crucial to find those moments when they are connected or when they may disagree with another character, but still make every *effort* to maintain rapport, prior to dropping any attempt and allowing the conflict full-out expression.

Phone rapport

Actors often need to make cold calls related to seeking work, so using your voice/speech skills in isolation is crucial. Here, however is a more universal real life example.

> Imagine you are calling your doctor's office for an appointment.
> The receptionist answers "Edgwood Clinic. This is Becky."
> Not so great reply (neutral tone) "I need to set up an appointment."

Now this *is* what you are calling for, but consider establishing rapport and then making Becky's life easier.

> Better reply (in a pleasant, engaging tone) "Good morning Becky. This is Robert Barton. I need to set up an appointment for a physical with Dr. Seidel for next month. It would

need to be on a Tuesday or Thursday afternoon, if that is possible."

You have acknowledged her by name and actually greeted her. She is likely to be bringing your file up and the doctor's schedule as you are speaking and you have answered almost all the questions she would in the first scenario be forced to ask.

So imagine you have now completed the transaction.
Not so great ending: "OK, thanks."

(If you are not good at remembering names, write hers down when she first answers, since you already have paper and pencil at hand to record your appointment.)

Better ending: "Thanks a lot Becky. I will see you on October second at two. Bye."

Again you have acknowledged her as a person with a name, not just a filter, and have confirmed that you got the appointment info right. Cautionary note: some people overdo the use of a stranger's name in a transparent attempt at achieving rapport. Better generally to restrict using it to the beginning and end of the conversation.

The above encounter has no V and no K, so your A awareness needs to be very much in place, with your voice alive, engaged and responsive. Whenever one of the three is cut off, we need to employ a measure of compensation

Life provides a great and fun laboratory for rapport building in every single interaction. Actors have brief opportunities with other auditioners and those who are running try-outs, with other cast members, costume shop personnel, publicity staff, photographers, crew and various other production staff members. Stepping outside the theatre, we have mini-improvised scenes at gas stations, banks, grocery stores, post offices, restaurants, to name just a few. If we can reframe each of these from *business as usual* to *a brief but empathetic human connection*, the encounter will not only go more smoothly but it will also be infinitely more satisfying. If you up your rapport antennae and help others feel more comfortable around you, the benefits are immeasurable.

In our theatre arts department at the University of Oregon, we are blessed to have a wonderfully capable and compassionate office supervisor May-Britt Jeremiah, who has a sign prominently placed on her desk which reads:

> Be kinder than is necessary, for everyone you meet is fighting some kind of battle.

Imagine what our lives would be like if instead of framing others as "someone I need to deal with," we tried "someone who can really use kindness from me, because they have enough battles to fight already."

Summary

In reframing experiences, perceptions and events, we can make each of them work more effectively for us. It is a way of developing empathy between those with inclinations to strongly opposing modalities. Often the simple choice of a different word or term can reframe perception. A variety of warm-ups can take us out of reliance on consciousness to the power of our unconscious mind to move us towards resolution. The core states we all seek can be summoned to ready access. VAK added to any new encounter can make names and facts easier to remember. Recognizing metaprograms and metalanguage tendencies can provide personal insight and enhance the process of characterization.

Reframing our perception of the process of rapport can make it far easier to achieve both in person and on the phone. It is as important to be able to break rapport as it is to establish it. Our opportunities to master it are limitless.

Words to remember

comparison
complex necessity and
    equivalence
core states
faulty cause and effect
faulty presupposition
general/specific
internal/external
judgment
match/mismatch
meditation
metalanguage
metaprograms
Mind Juggling

mind reading
nominalizations
partner breathing
polarity words
proactive/reactive
rapport
reframing
towards/away
transformative vocabulary
trunk packing
unspecified nouns and
    pronouns
unspecified verbs
VAK conjuring

5

NLP SCENE STUDY

I hear, and I forget. I see, and I remember. I do, and I understand.

Chinese proverb

The initial stages of scene study should be traditional preparation, stemming from your past actor training and involving character analysis, staging, memorization and rehearsal processes that you learned prior to experiencing this book and widely available in others. While NLP communication skills can enhance and provide insights as you move through each of these stages, the integration of actual NLP processes is most beneficial later when the basic components are in place. NLPing a scene can be effective earlier in the process, but my recommendation is to go through your usual process and then bring in NLP to kick out the jams or to breathe new life into your work. As the proverb above implies, no matter what one's modality preference, the strongest loading comes from kinesthetic exposure.

After a scene has been presented and critiqued in a familiar way, the following elements may be added. If it is possible to have two sets of actors working on the same scene, the opportunities for NLP exploration are even greater, as will come clear in upcoming exercises.

Character analysis

The first step, once you have completed the standard character analysis (given circumstances, super-objective, through-line of actions, etc.) taught in most acting classes and traditionally used in rehearsal, is to enhance that information by completing the following statements and answering subsequent questions. This will add richness and possibility to those you have already answered. (NOTE: The NLP-style character analysis form is in Appendix C.)

- The character:

    - looks like me
    - does not look like me
    - sounds like me
    - does not sound like me
    - feels like me
    - does not feel like me.

- Changes I most need to make are:
- To my character:

    - the world looks
    - the world sounds
    - the world feels, smells, tastes like.

- The most significant impression my character makes in each modality is:
- My character's primary VAK mode is:
- Major shifts/synesthesia take place when:
- *Meta-model* tendencies and examples include:

    - unspecified nouns and pronouns
    - unspecified verbs
    - nominalizations
    - polarity words
    - mind reading.

- *Core states* achieved and out of reach?
- *Metaprograms* pattern tendencies:

- • proactive/reactive
- • towards/away
- • internal/external
- • options/procedures
- • general/specific
- • match/mismatch.

- • *Rapport*: My character and the other:

  - • are most in rapport when:
  - • are least in rapport when:
  - • As actors, we need to be most in rapport when:

- • The positive intentions behind my character's most repre-hensible behavior are:
- • If I could NLP my character, I would:
- • *Characterization*: The answers above that will influence the way I portray this character most significantly are:

Rehearsal explorations

Just as understanding the character can be expanded and deep-ened by the analysis above, bringing the text further to life and engaging your partner more dynamically can come from the exercises below. Some of these are not unique to NLP, but when pursued through NLP (particularly VAK) filters, can offer new perspectives and insights.

Subtext

Subtext is an actor's air. Finding, changing and shading subtext is what actors love to do and what audiences most love to watch. Stanislavski says that *subtext* is what the audience comes to the theatre to see, that if all they wanted was the *text* they could have stayed home and read the script. Subtext is a phenomenal source of power. It may totally alter text.

The problem many actors experience is that they are too used to writing formally in perfect sentences. Subtext is actually often jagged, incomplete, interrupted thoughts, with illogical twists and turns. The language (because it doesn't need censoring) may be rough, crude, irrational, profane, even silly. Your interior monolog is a recording that runs continuously in your head, and when you are scattered or disorganized, it is doubly so. No one's is tidy. Because this stuff is unspoken, and *behind* the words, it is often quite socially unacceptable, which is why we usually don't say it.

Spoken silent script

Speak your continuous subtext in addition to the text. Recognize inner thoughts and get them into words. Overlap with your partner, as needed as your recordings run simultaneously. Speak the "silent" parts with less projected volume than the actual lines. You will find out where your thinking has been muddy and achieve clarity.

Shadowing

This exercise works particularly well if two sets of actors are working on the same scene, but can be done where one set has viewed the scene previously.

Hand two other actors your scripts, and have them go through the scene reading the lines. You and your partner shadow them, telling them where to move, asking to have some words punched, to repeat some lines or moves, with greater emphasis, encouraging before an important moment, praising them after a maneuver is accomplished successfully, acting as alter ego and coach. When you are ready for your "stand-in" to read the line, press her lightly on the shoulder as a signal. If you want her to stop in the middle of a line, do the same.

History

First meeting of the characters

Set up all the circumstances of the first time the two of you laid eyes on each other. Then enter the scene from a point of innocence and discover your partner. Leave the encounter when you have some idea when you will see this person again. Let this memory be highly VAK loaded and influence the scene itself.

Crucial offstage event

Select the single most influential experience, either before the play begins or away from the script, on your actions in it. This may or may not involve your partner. Set yourself up simply to respond without scripting the experience. Since this moment was life-changing for your character, it will provide a reference point, that can reverberate during key moments within the scene itself.

Moment before

Most scenes begin with characters entering or with someone leaving the characters onstage. In the former instance, establish exactly what, when, where and why you are entering. If possible start the scene some distance from the acting area, engaging in the dialogue that would have preceded it. This allows you to enter with all cylinders kicking, instead of starting cold. Remember, we are experiencing a phase in these characters' lives, just picking it up in a moment in time. Find all the conditioning forces (time, temperature, space familiarity, mood, distractions, light) that will add texture and detail to the entrance itself. Enter with all your cylinders running.

Half hour before

Rewind to a full 30 minutes before the scene, to experience all the same elements and to provide a sense of immediate history. Ask yourself if some inciting event may have occurred that actually causes the scene to happen. If this was a shared experience, actually improvise it and plant certain stimuli that may come to fruition in the body of the scene.

Perspective

Role reversal

Switch parts with your partner and run the scene. Carry the script if needed but be as free of it as possible. Keep the major shape of the scene the same, but feel free to use your own line readings and character business whenever you wish to do something differently.

Listen closely to your partner when he gives a new and interesting twist to a speech, when it sounds the same as the way you usually do it, when your sense of timing is altered. Notice when he comes up with an interesting piece of business or variation in the blocking. Enjoy playing the other role and doing all the things you might wish the other actor would do, but would never "direct" him to do. You learn how well you know the whole scene and how often you have simply been biding your time and not really listening when your partner speaks. It is also therapeutic to be able to say the words and do the other part the way you want. Whether or not your partner hears, notices or decides to use anything of yours, at least you've had the chance. You tend to feel freer, find places where you may have been making your partner wait too long, have been anticipating his cues, or business you have been making more difficult than necessary. Most of all, you have a huge boost of empathy for your partner, having walked in his shoes.

A different partner

(This is another exercise that can be invaluable when two sets of actors have been working on the same scene and have been employing the same basic set.)

Without any preparation, present the scene, not with the person with whom you have been rehearsing but with the other actor playing her role or a classmate standing in. You will need to calibrate fully because, while you know what lines the other actor will deliver, you do not know how or where she will be in the space. You will need all your VAK awareness. You will need to really see, hear, sense and feel, and be completely alive and alert. Great acting seems to be happening for the first time. This provides you with that sensation in an amazing and compelling way. Take this powerful loading back into your work with your regular scene partner, forgetting what you know will happen, connecting moment by moment, and allowing yourself to be surprised.

Handicaps

Many beginning acting classes do a blind exercise, where one actor leads a blindfolded partner around the building and outside, guiding her carefully and encouraging the touching of various surfaces. By the end of the exercise, the "blind" actor is hearing, smelling, tasting, and feeling sensations on a greatly enhanced level. Just as people who have permanently lost the use of one sense tend to develop compensatory sensory acuity in the others, whenever an actor limits V, A or K, the result tends to kick the others up several notches. Adding some limitation to the scene can sharpen the intensity of communication in other areas and get both actors thinking again.

Back to back

Play the scene sitting back to back, with your partner's arms and yours locked at the elbows and neither of you having any possibility of seeing the other. Communicate everything through your voice and whatever pressure you can manage on the other person's back and your arms, where looped. This gooses your auditory awareness and expressiveness in line delivery, while the contact gives you a strong sense of what the other person is feeling and a specific kinesthetic channel to communicate back your own feelings.

Space to fill

Sit against the wall, facing each other at opposite ends of a large classroom or rehearsal hall. Communicate over the vast space, keeping the scene intimate and complex, not allowing it to become just loud and flat. Feel the powerful need to connect over the divide between you. Not only can this enhance line readings, but it can ease you into the controlled but powerful projection you often need to fill a performance space.

Radio show

Imagine your scene as radio drama or a recorded book CD. The listening audience will only be able to experience the action with their ears, so your inflections, non-verbals and specific line readings need to have enough clarity to compensate. This will really get you working on shaping your line readings for interesting and evocative shadings, thereby providing another way to bump the auditory component of your performance up more than a few notches. We all tend to believe we are doing more vocally, making more interesting shifts in pitch, contrasting the big stressed phrases with those we throw away, putting forth variety in volume, tone, tempo and rhythm. Then we listen to recordings and go "Hmmm … I'm not doing as much as I thought I was." So taping simply gives you permission to do more, with more vocal peaks and valleys. Record and playback enough times to be satisfied that this is the richest listening experience possible.

Run scene with sound track playing

Now that you have the recording, rehearse the scene with it running, so you do not have to deliver your lines. Communicate with your eyes and your body, not to overcompensate for not speaking, but in a relaxed mode of discovery. Because you have now been temporarily freed from the A obligation of the scene, you can be way more open to V and K discoveries. Really look at your partner for any discoveries you may have missed by being too preoccupied by speaking the text.

Let your body tell you any new and interesting physical impulses and welcome any shifts in emotion that come when the words seem to be flowing through you without your having an obligation to speak. Hold these visual and kinesthetic memories when you return to regular spoken rehearsal.

Neutral masks

Run through the scene wearing neutral masks. The plain white plastic ones that are often part of a theatre department arsenal or are available at most theatrical supply stores will work fine. Suddenly your reliance on using your facial expressions and studying those of your partner are no longer options. Now you have cut off a crucial V component. However, you may find yourself noticing far more how your partner is using her body, reading gestures and basic moves more clearly so you are upping another V stimulus at the same time. You may find yourself discovering new movements yourself (K) and both exploring new line readings and attending more sharply to those of your partner (A).

Kino loading

Contact

Touch your partner at some point during each of your lines in the scene. Take your time. Find some way to physically connect with her every time you speak, anything from traditional moves (patting on the shoulder, nudging, pointing into someone's upper chest) to those that are discovered (touching elbows, pulling someone's shirt untucked, even pressing your nose to someone's knee). Some combination of the conventional and the new will emerge. Let your body and your emotions tell you some way to connect at the same time your words do. A surprising number of these moves end up being serious possibilities to put into the actual scene. Others provide an emotional memory for the body to suppress interestingly later. Emotional contact is heightened by physical contact and unexpectedly sharper line readings are often discovered. It is amazing how often the pure kinesthetic experience of the touch, once experienced, but then cut back, will somehow feed into auditory expressiveness.

Passing

Start with a simple object, such as a rubber ball, beanbag or tennis ball, and run the scene, passing it to the other person at the very end of each speech. Use the object to punctuate your lines while you have it, and literally pass it to your partner the way the cue is passed (violently, slyly, flirtatiously, with outrage, with joy and so on). Let the relationship between the characters centre in the object. Remember you don't just have to hand it to the other person, you can put it in his pocket, on his head, throw it to him. You can nudge it over to him with your foot or your little pinkie. You can do more than hold it while you speak. You can crush it, roll it or juggle it. Try this also with a stuffed animal or doll that has somewhat more of an identity than the neutral object. Again, the passing helps punch your delivery, which often remains at that level later.

Variation: Find a game that is appropriate to the conflict in the scene (ping-pong if it is fast, witty repartee, boxing if it is all frontal assault, chess if it is sly and calculated) and explore the same way. As the energy goes into the object, it also goes into the words, so variety and clarity both rise. Individual consonants and vowels, within words, get more liveliness and variety of attack. Both partners become more alert in hearing and receiving cues.

Key searching

Actors often report that they were searching and searching ("And then I just put on this scarf and that was the key.") when suddenly the door to the whole characterization opened. A costume piece, prop, some pronounced physical characteristic or vocal tendency will be so strongly right as to unlock some important doors. A simple physical object or tiny change can suddenly make you feel like another human being, with detail after detail rushing in to complete the character.

Here are V, A and K examples, just to bump your imagination:

Visual	Auditory	Kinesthetic
a hat	humming frequently	the set of your jaw
a handkerchief	a startling, explosive laugh	hands thrust deep in your pockets
a pair of shoes	a nasal vocal quality	feet turned out as you walk
glasses	punching key consonants	darting, indirect contact
a scarf	a distinct regional accent	walking with heel pressure

Explore your own residence (and, if available, your theatre's prop room or costume storage area), trying things on, picking up, handling, examining small objects, letting each work on the character's sense of self. Keep your personal antennae out everywhere you go for objects that might open character doors. Do the same thing with isolated physical and vocal characteristics and techniques. Try them on, seeing if they fit (or even release) the character.

Note that keys may often be present in how you relate to items that have already been provided. In the first list above, it may be the discovery of *exactly how* – the exact angle at which you will wear the hat, or how often you will take out and wipe your hands on the handkerchief, the fact that you never tie your shoe laces, vainly take off your glasses when encountering strangers, or drop and misplace your scarf every time you start to leave.

VAK experiments

In Chapter 3, we explored how a single monolog could be shaken and stirred by simply deciding the character was V, A or K or selecting moments of transition between modalities. This can be even more effective in partner work.

1   Rehearse the scene with:

- both characters Vs
- both characters As
- both characters Ks.

Taking the scene way into each modality. This will feel extreme but that very thing can help you then find where the characters are shifting modalities and where they definitely are not.

2   One character is V and the other K for an entire run-through, then the other way around for maximum conflict. Because these two modalities tend to have maximum conflict/contrast in life, and conflict is so vital to drama, it can punch up that element in the scene itself.

3   The above assignments, but with a crucial moment where characters switch modalities. The shifting dynamic might be intriguingly heightened if, at a crucial moment, instead of joining each other, you simply slip into the other person's modality.

4   One actor stays in a single modality while the other changes continuously. This can be particularly useful if one is consistent and perhaps stubborn, while the other is mercurial and chameleon. It can be particularly effective if one character is continually trying, but failing, to pin the other down.

5   VAK schizoids, where both characters continuously drift in and out of modalities, but are never in the same one at the same time. This can enhance a context where characters constantly almost connect and then just miss each other, a series of close calls and missed moments. An effective variation is to have very brief moments where the characters land in the same modality and just as they are about to feel relieved and comfortable, they again fall out.

6   Structure a scene for VAK sequence where both actors change at the same moment. In the same way there is dynamic energy in the shifts offered by the Best Day of My Life monolog assignment, if two characters shift at the same time, it can be a wonderful way of having them go on the same journey. In a flirtation or courtship scene, for example, the character might begin as tentative visuals with nervous interaction, relax into auditories enjoying each other's conversation, and then experience a big kino release when they acknowledge their mutual attraction and kiss or embrace.

7   Rapport shifting. Run the entire scene:

- totally out of rapport
- moving in and out of rapport
- totally in rapport.

This may release some clues previously not apparent or some stronger choices, such as when characters are experiencing a huge chasm of understanding and accord but are striving mightily to stay in rapport in order to preserve the relationship.

Finding anchors in the scene

You will recall that an anchor is a fairly intense response that has been planted (anchored) by some past experience and which we tend to repeat automatically in similar circumstances thereafter. (NOTE: The Find the Anchors Form is Appendix D.)
    Ask yourself which anchors may be present in:

architectural elements – furniture – hand props – clothing – jewelry – grooming – facial expressions – gestures – movements – physical proximity or touch – sounds – non-verbals – words or phrases – tone of voice – timing

Try to find at least one positive and one negative anchor in:

1   the acting space
2   your partner's physical behavior
3   what your partner says or how she says it
4   for each character a moment when a new anchoring takes place during the scene itself.

You may wish to share some anchors you have discovered in the scene, but then keep others to yourself, just as the character would.

Monolog solo work

All the preceding work requires the presence of a partner. If you are working a monolog alone, there are ways of tweaking it suggested in Chapters 2 and 3. With the exercises above you can still employ:

- NLP character analysis
- speaking subtext
- imagining/reliving a crucial offstage event
- establishing the moment before
- recording as if for radio broadcast
- running the speech without speaking it, but with recording playing
- playing with an object to up emphasis, without actually passing it
- key searching
- experimenting with rapport with your imaginary listener(s)
- finding, shifting anchors.

Monolog partner work

If you are fortunate enough to be working a monolog and have a partner for that purpose, two exercises can be extremely helpful.

Contact with the speech

Monologs often begin with the character answering some kind of inquiry or challenge, perhaps taking your turn to speak in a group setting, taking a stand because you disagree with something that has been said, or reacting to your imaginary partner's attitude which motivates you to speak. Too often the actor just starts, not taking time for this cue-in event to happen. Decide on the exact moment before and have your partner, standing out in the audience, actually cue you in. Because your audience will never hear this line when you eventually present the speech in a class or audition, you may choose a challenging, button-pushing remark that is not actually in the script but really gets you reactive and motivated. Load the memory strongly enough that you have no trouble playing the cue when you are no longer actually receiving it.

Push, pull, hug

This is a deeply kinesthetic exercise that can provide you with all kinds of powerful physical memories to assist in upping the impact of your delivery long after the process is over.

Push. One actor pushes the other from behind with the pushee (receiver) resisting but not so much that the action is truly difficult. The pushee may change directions, trying to escape but does not try to leave the space. The pusher may vary the intensity, timing and force of the push, sustaining a level that helps "push the buttons" of the pushee, but is never fierce enough to be in any way physically painful.

Pull. One actor takes the other's hands and pulls her around the room, often in circles or curves, sometimes in straight lines, possibly moving down into a crouched position or up on tiptoes, but rarely stopping movement. The emotional context that emerges may be joyous, teasing, taunting or whatever seems to emerge from the activity.

Hug. Both actors sit on the floor, close, one in front of the other, with one embracing the other from behind and providing affectionate contact (somewhat like the *Pietà* sculpture) throughout the speech. The hug is constant but may again vary in intensity or the degree to which the hugee is actually enveloped by the hugger.

Each actor experiences push, pull, and hug as both speaker and non-speaker. Suggested sequence:

1   A speaks, pushes B
2   B speaks, pushes A
3   A speaks, is pushed by B
4   B speaks, is pushed by A.
5   A speaks, pulls B
6   B speaks, pulls A
7   A speaks, is pulled by B

  8   B speaks, is pulled by A
  9   A speaks, hugs B
 10   B speaks, hugs A
 11   A speaks, is hugged by B
 12   B speaks, is hugged by A.

After steps 4, 8, and 12, stop for a breather (the first two sets can get a bit strenuous) and discuss any discoveries you may have made, before moving on.

This exercise can invoke and unlock a wide range of kinesthetic responses both physically and emotionally. If you are working on a scene where one or both of you have a speech of some length, doing this isolation work can be equally powerful for that part of the scene.

All the analyses and exercises in this chapter can shake up the scene in a good way, adding freshness and discovery. While you can benefit by trying them all, if you are working under constraints of time, consider selecting processes based on a diagnostic of your needs as actors and on places where the scene is simply not as strong as you would like after the first time it is presented and critiqued. So, for example, if it is the speaking of the text that seems like the weak link, focus on exercises that isolate and expand the auditory component. I urge you to try them all, but if that is not practical, determine your needs, select from the overall menu and then NLP them.

Summary

After a scene has been worked in a traditional way, blending in approaches to shake up the process through NLP filters can be a great supplement and enhancement. It can expand the ways characters may be revealed. Exercises can explore and heighten subtext, reveal the past histories of characters which influence present behavior, and shake up each actor's perspective. By shutting off V, A or K elements, the scene can be revealed in new ways. Each modality can be enriched by temporarily cutting off the others. Keys to entering a character's life may be powerful impulses from the modalities. Multiple experiments in scene rehearsal include shifting rapport, finding anchors and isolating key speeches for further intensified exploration. Coming at a scene from all possible directions is highly recommended, but if conditions require it, select rehearsal experiments based on where the work needs stimulus.

Words/exercises to remember

back to back
character history
contact on every line
contact with the speech
crucial offstage event
a different partner
first meeting of the characters
half hour before
handicaps
key searching
kino loading
moment before
neutral masks

passing
push, pull, hug
radio show
role reversal
scene anchors
scene with sound track
shadowing
space to fill
spoken silent script
VAK experiments

6

GETTING IT DONE

Knowing is not enough. We must apply. Willing is not enough.
We must do.

Goethe

In previous chapters, we have dealt with ways NLP can help work
through personal issues, clarifying thinking and freeing up motivation. We have also examined it as a supplement to the rehearsal
process. In this last chapter, we will focus on how NLP can provide
shortcuts, ways to get there faster, avoiding road bumps and detours.

Chunking

When overwhelmed about how to move swiftly forward on
something, we may need to "chunk" it. The term originated in
the field of Information Technology (IT) dealing with chunks of
information. There are three ways to chunk: up, down or sideways. Here is a simple visual sample:

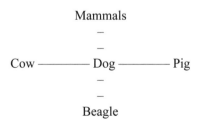

We go up to a larger, more universal context or to see "the big picture." We need to do that when we "can't see the forest for the trees." We go down when stuck, don't know what to do next (or first), and need to take "baby steps." We may go up to remind ourselves how much we love someone and down to begin to demonstrate that in concrete ways because "love is in the details." Chunking up we look through a telescope, down through a microscope. Most of us know how to chunk, as evidenced by all the phrases above that are in common usage, but it is also an option many of us forget, while wasting time. Sometimes we need to move from the specific to the general or from the part to the whole and sometimes we need to do the exact opposite.

Chunking sideways involves moving across a topic to a parallel universe of some kind, a substitute which may be similar or a synonym that may stand in for the more literal experience. It can be useful when you are too close to the issue, but can gain insights by looking at something similar where you are less emotionally entangled. It can be very effective when you are not succeeding at present but can move sideways to other areas where you *have* had success to determine what you can learn from those and take back as resources in your current situation. Or you may feel trapped in the precise, verbatim version of your experience, but more open to taking it into metaphor.

To give the best possible performance an actor needs to do all three. You chunk up to determine your character's super-objective and your overall objective in each scene. This gives you a sense of purpose and helps tie your performance into a unified whole. It is not, however, effective to dwell on these in performance, because while a super-objective may provide motivation and even inspiration, it does not get you moving in specific ways. Instead, you can move through what are some-times called beats, in which you chunk your performance down into the smallest possible motivational units where every action has an intention.

Here is an excerpt from an open scene scenario from my book *Acting: Onstage and Off*. The dialogue is incredibly simple:

1. Oh.	2. Nothing.
2. Yes.	1. Listen.
1. Why are you doing this?	2. No.
2. It's the best thing.	1. Oh.
1. You can't mean it.	2. You're good.
2. No, I'm serious.	1. Forget it.
1. Please.	2. What?
2. What?	1. Go on.
1. What does this mean?	2. I will.

The setting is a bedroom, the characters a young married couple

The couple lost their only child before the baby reached age three. The tragic death occurred about six months before. Lately the wife has often been found sobbing hysterically over the child's basket of toys. The day has come when the husband is determined to get rid of the toys, because of the way they continue to haunt his wife and himself.

There are only five brief lines but 16 beats, seven of them occurring before any dialogue is spoken. Breaking down the performance into these specific moment-to-moment chunks prevents the performer from feeling overwhelmed, makes the task entirely possible and the acting clear and precise.

To make sure a performance is complex and varied, or simply to break out of a rut, the actor will often chunk sideways to "abstract" the character. The classic example is to ask if this character were an animal, what would she be and then to incorporate some of those animal details into the performance. This is particularly effective if your work so far lacks a kinesthetic edge, if it is insufficiently spontaneous, earthy or sensual. Other abstractions include identifying the character as fabric, beverage, mode of transportation, city, tree or vegetation, color, play/film, scent, type of day, decade or era, song, mythological or fantasy figure, landmark or building, snack, spice or flavor, musical instrument, painting or photo, or toy, all of which can provide a sideways way of shaking up your performance.

Abstraction can also be an invaluable tool for rehearsal interaction, removing a conversation from blunt or potentially embarrassing exchanges. When the legendary actor John Gielgud was playing King Lear, his director Clive Barker said to him "Lear

Time to let go

Activity		Intention
1	She enters bedroom	*To find something to distract her*
2	She finds and opens a book	*To grab first available diversion*
3	She sits on bed	*To calm herself*
4	She pages through the book	*To occupy her mind*
5	She hears noise, starts, recovers	*To suppress her fears*
6	She crosses to the door	*To somehow stop what she expects*
7	He enters with basket	*To make her understand his plan*
8	She says, "Oh"	*To get him to stop*
9	He says, "Yes"	*To make her understand that it is time to do this*
10	She touches the toys	*To somehow touch her child as well*
11	She asks, "Why are you doing this?"	*To cause him to change his mind*
12	He says, "It's the best thing"	*To get her to admit they need to do it*
13	She takes the basket	*To stay close to the toys*
14	She says, "You can't mean it"	*To intimidate him*
15	She kneels, puts toys on the floor	*To keep them near her*
16	He moves to put a hand on her shoulder	*To comfort her*

should be an oak: you're an ash; now we've got to do something about that." This was a masterful abstract. Gielgud, while brilliant, was not ideally cast. Lear is a man who has been extraordinarily powerful, a true warrior, or to use another sideways chunk, "an old lion." Of living actors, Sean Connery would be an ideal choice. Gielgud was an actor of great delicacy and refinement, his essential impression that of an esthete. If the director had chosen to be uncomfortably brusque, he might have said something like "John, you're just too soft and feminine for this role. You need to play it with some power and guts. So stop it with the limp wrists and give me some balls." Unfortunately, more than a few directors communicate exactly like that. Instead Barker chose to chunk sideways into the world of trees and he communicated the same information in a way that was respectful and far easier for the recipient to hear.

In their careers, actors often find themselves strategically chunking. Partly because this is one of the professions with the largest unemployment statistics in the world, you may need to frequently chunk up to asking yourself why you really want to be an actor, what you hope to gain from it, what you want ultimately to contribute, what it means to you to be a part of this art. If you can answer those to your satisfaction, then you may chunk way down to steps you can begin to take today to move your career forward. If you have felt stuck, these need to be small and manageable enough that they essentially become the next 'beats' of your pursuit of the life of an actor.

If you have been turned down a number of times recently or had opportunities fall through and are in danger of feeling like a failure, you may elect to chunk sideways to some recent successes in order to take some of that confidence and energy with you the next time you have an interview or go on rounds.

If, in your metaprogram self-analysis, in the general/specific category, if you have a strong tendency to go general, you need to learn to chunk way down to take those great ideas and implement them. If you tend to go specific, you may need to move up when you need excitement, inspiration and a more sweeping overview. Just as all actors benefit from full VAK mastery, so also are they well served by being able to instantly chunk in any direction. A great filmmaker knows just when to go out for a wide panoramic shot, when to go in for a tight close-up and when to change the angle of the shot altogether. So should you in the imaginary film of your personal epic called "My Life."

Core Transformation

One of the most profound NLP processes, Core Transformation was developed by Connirae Andreas and is fully explored in the book of that title, co-written with her sister Tamora. If you Google the topic, you can access numerous sites and view demonstration DVDs modeling the process. NLP institutes sometimes offer one- to three-day seminars on this process alone. If it intrigues you after this discussion, do consider investigating more (the book and demonstration DVD are in the "Further study" suggestions at the end of the text) and enrolling for such training, as it is far more effective if done with a trained guide.

Remember the core states from the warm-up section in Chapter 4? This process helps one return to these as well as others such as wholeness, grace, fullness, enlightenment, completeness, comfort, awareness, depth, power, radiance, transcendence as well as feeling aware, in touch, open, centered, fluid, attuned, present, compassionate, radiant and welcoming. Not bad, huh? Most of us would be quite willing and motivated to have and feel all of the above. I have observed participants break through in just a few hours blocks that have been haunting them for many years.

Connirae Andreas began to develop this process after a week-long group visit with Milton Erickson during the last year of his life, where he was able to help her make an enormous personal transformation very swiftly without even speaking directly to her. This made her realize that it was possible to achieve a sense of complete well-being in a very short period of time.

The Core Transformation process reveals in a highly graceful way that what you perceive as limitations in your life can actually be doorways toward resolution, that your personal darkness can be a source of light. It starts with something you dislike about yourself, identifying a feeling or behavior that is keeping you from moving forward. An example might be that, as an actor, you have been longing to start taking some risks in your work. At the same time, as a person, you have been wanting to take more chances in your life encounters. But something always makes you stop. So, instead, your performances continue to involve safe, perhaps bland, perhaps even boring choices, and your relationships lack depth and excitement. A part of you just will not let you risk.

You begin by acknowledging and thanking that part for caring enough about you to so fiercely influence you. This can be as difficult as expressing gratitude to someone who gives you harsh criticism. But, as we discussed in Chapter 1, such a person has to, on some level, care about you simply to take the time and energy to put forth the criticism, when it would be so much easier to avoid the confrontation. So you start by honoring this part of you for being concerned on some level for your welfare.

Then you ask it to tell you what its positive intention is for you, what it wants for you that makes it step up and prevent you from moving forward. You need to be patient and wait for an answer because you may not have communicated directly with this part of you before. You may have tried very hard to ignore it or reject it. Or you may have judged it, abused it and cursed it for stopping you. If you acknowledged it at all, you would have had an antagonistic relationship. So you put out the request with gratitude and respect. In the example above, when you get an answer, the part might reply that it wants to protect you. It wants to keep you from being hurt or rejected, wants to keep you safe from harm. You thank it for that and then ask "If I could have a strong sense of protection and just start with that, what do you want for me on an even deeper level?" You continue to ask and receive answers, for up to a half dozen levels, before you get to what the part wants most or its meta-outcome.

Finally you ask if you could have whatever this answer is, would the part be willing to allow you to explore more and generally the answer is yes. This is your core state. You may then go through a process of finding out how old the part is (and often it is very young and did not mature, which may explain in part why it has been so stubborn and inflexible, as it has been working with limited resources), then bringing it through your life up to your current age. You may work your way back through all the answers to gain approval. You may inquire if there are any other parts of you that object to your embracing this core state. You may also go through an embedding process much as if you have inherited this state (called Parental Timeline Imprinting) to establish it more deeply and allow it to spread through every pore of your being and every part of your past, present and projected future.

I began the process by dealing with a state I called "anticipation anxiety," being sometimes terrified of encounters with new people, challenging social occasions, generally being in groups where I did not know the others or exactly how to proceed. An actor having this kind of fear? Yes, because in the theatre I knew my lines and moves and I knew why the audience had come and that I could give them what they wanted. In these other situations I knew none of this. I had felt this anticipation anxiety strongly that very morning, fearing going to the Core Transformation seminar where I would be surrounded by 80 strangers and not knowing what to expect from any of them.

After going through all the stages and questions with my part, the final answer I got was "profound peace." That may seem, and with surprising frequency is, in direct opposition to my original state. While difficult to explain, I would say that part of me wanted me to stay home where I could experience peace and not go places where I could lose it. The process was helpful in allowing me simply to decide to tap into a place of "profound peace" before such events and I have rarely experienced that kind of anxiety since.

All I can offer is firsthand testimony and encourage you to pursue this process, because it is an ultimate short-cut to fulfillment. It is short, clear and frequently successful. Many participants have gotten results that eluded them throughout years and years of therapy. One of the classic NLP reframe images is of a small child approaching Michelangelo asking him why he was beating on an enormous piece of marble. His response was "because there is an angel inside that I need to let out." Great sculptures release wonders from slabs of stone. The Core Transformation process can unleash your angel from your rock.

Memorization strategies

NLP is all about modeling, finding someone who is really good at something and then figuring out what parts of what they do the rest of us can emulate. Satir, Perls and Erickson were modeled for communication/healing brilliance. Gandhi and Mother Teresa were modeled for contagious peace strategies. I would be amazed if someone is not studying Oprah for communication power as well as financial acumen. And I hope someone is studying Meryl Streep for acting strategies.

One important study that should be done but as yet has not, is modeling those who memorize lines swiftly and efficiently. Some actors are quick studies and others are painfully slow. There is a definite trend to ask for lines earlier and earlier in rehearsal. So in the "getting it done" focus of this chapter, many actors can use some strategies for memorization.

There *has* been a music study done on those who commit songs to memory quickly. The results were that they all:

- assumed the same posture, head tilted to one side, eyes downward while listening the first time they heard the song. They described this has getting an overall "feeling," "mood" or "imprint."
- formed a visual representation, always some kind of graph with a vertical axis for pitch, horizontal or time, but not necessarily like sheet music. Their "pictures" were quite individualistic.

So, in addition to the auditory listening component, they got a feeling for the music and a detailed image, adding K and V to the A. The more difficult the song, the more important the musicians reported the K and V components were to mastery. After this initial loading of modalities, they all also:

- then reran the music in their heads
- then sang it at a much faster tempo than it was written
- then performed the song in the original mode, which one singer described as "hearing the picture of the feeling of the tune."

Here is how one of the greatest musicians of all time described how he worked:

> This fires my soul, and provided I am not disturbed, my subject enlarges itself, becomes defined, and the whole, even if it is long, stands nearly complete and finished in my mind, so that I can survey it like a fine picture or a beautiful statue at a glance. Nor do I hear in my mind the parts successively, but I hear them all at once, along with a powerful range of feelings. What a delight this is!
>
> (Mozart, 1789)

So, based on the study above and other elements of NLP, here are some tips. Remember the name trunk exercise from the

118

warm-up section in Chapter 4, which works for a whole group to learn each other's names quickly? In this case, even if you tend to be a V, A or K, you want to embrace them all. If you have trouble getting lines down, try the following.

Scenes and monologs

1   Highlight lines, rather than underlining them; this can make the lines seem to jump off the page and make a more vivid impression on your memory.
2   Memorize according to what the character *wants*, not words by rote. Memorize thought and intention clusters rather than word clusters. Actors who forget or "go up" on lines have just placed the words in their heads, with narrow computer logic, so that when the word is gone, so are they.
3   Get up on your feet and move in some way to load the words in after you have memorized them. If the scene has been blocked, go through your exact movements and lock the words in direct association with your staging as you speak them.
4   Place a card over your upcoming lines and reveal only as much to yourself as absolutely necessary as you cue yourself and master each line.
5   Use images to get a vivid film and/or still shot to associate with each group of words. The visual as it pops back into your mind will tend to bring the lines with it. Add sharp physical and emotional sensations on key words as well.
6   Vary the tempo-rhythm with which you run the lines so you are open to different attacks in rehearsal. This will also make it less likely that you will forget when some surprise comes up during rehearsal that might tend to break your rhythm and concentration there.
7   Every other day, run through lines as fast as you can without losing sense or emotional connection. You will find places where you can speed up in performance, but, more importantly, doing it fast can solidify the words in your head.

For scenes

1   Start memorizing from your *cues*, not from the first word of your lines. Memorize at least the last half of your partner's speeches and listen closely as they near the end of each. Do not become one of those actors who are paralyzed because they were not expecting their partners to stop talking.
2   Cue yourself off motivating words (action cues) within your partner's speeches, the words that stimulate response, not off the last word (line cue) of his speech. Start gearing up to respond on a word or phrase while the other person is still talking.
3   Buy a small hand-held recorder that will fit in a pocket and that you can take anywhere. Tape record your partner's lines with spaces to run yours or, if your partner is feeling helpful, have her tape her lines, so you can run yours when she's not around but still wish to hear the right voice, giving you cues.
4   Make a second recording of both your parts. This allows you to listen to a complete text while doing other tasks (driving, shaving, getting dressed) so you can let the words act on you without having to stop other activities. It also allows you to walk through your blocking without having to speak, which can enhance your sense of subtext.
5   Use flash cards, with the other actor's lines on one side and yours on the other. Putting the cards together takes time, but the act of writing them can speed memorization.
6   Wherever you are running lines, set up furniture so that it is close to your set and act walk through your blocking, even looking at the empty space where your partner would be and endowing it with her presence.

For monologs

1   Divide the speech into parts. Most have three to five. A subject might be introduced, a solution or two or three might be considered, and then some kind of conclusion might be made so the speech falls into a reaction–exploration–decision pattern. The parts may be places where you achieve

new realizations. There is always a structure that can be subdivided into smaller manageable chunks.

2   Record the speech a half dozen times in succession so that you can just let the player keep running and the words float over you while you go about some other task.

3   Highlight crucial words, using different colors for key verbs, nouns or important modifiers. Get a strong image of what these key words look like on the page.

4   Run your speech while doing some physical exercise, such as jogging or riding an exercise bike. Rhythm and exertion can help load in the words, as you multi-task.

5   Whenever you get stuck on a particular line or phrase, take time to give it an extra dose of visual and kinesthetic information. Make sure you have a highly vivid picture as well as a powerful sensation, an emotion, a physical impulse, a scent, a taste, a temperature – anything that can reinforce your memory of the line kinesthetically.

Using presuppositions

A presupposition is an implicit assumption whose truth is taken for granted in discourse.

Examples: If I say "Do you have to do it again?" the presupposition is that you have done it before, at least once. If I say "Lola no longer writes porn," the presupposition is that she at one time wrote porn. Many presuppositions come from a place of ignorance and confusion. The metalanguage patterns in Chapter 4 focus on fallible presuppositions and ways to help someone break through them. It is very upsetting when someone says something to you that presupposes something that is simply not right or that never happened.

But presuppositions can also be incredibly useful as filters on the world. Here is a list of some NLP presuppositions, which are not inherent truths, but productive ways to think:

1   The map is not the territory.
2   People respond according to their internal maps.
3   Meaning depends on understanding context.

4   Mind and body affect each other.
5   We need to respect each person's model of the world.
6   We are all more than our behavior.
7   Every behavior is useful in some context.
8   We cannot not communicate.
9   The meaning of your communication is the response you get.
10 Failure can be turned into feedback.
11 Whoever has the most flexibility exercises the most influence.
12 Anything can be accomplished if chunked down enough.
13 We all have the internal resources we need to succeed.
14 Communication should increase choice.
15 People make the best choices available to them at the time.

Now you may disagree with some of these statements, but remember I did not say they were true, but simply useful ways to think and very likely to allow you to move forward and get it done.

Here are some explanations of four presuppositions particularly relevant to the life of an actor in and out of the theatre:

The meaning of your communication is the response you get

If it isn't working try something else. This is a special message to parents (or directors) who say "How many times do I need tell you ...? Or to actors who say to their partners or directors "I keep asking you ... [fill in whatever], but I get nothing," who keep asking for the same help, the same way. How many times? Countless, because you are repeating something that didn't work. One might answer might be "Forever or a gazillion times unless you tell me differently or show me or frame it in some way that helps me respond." I would take the three strikes approach as the maximum repetition of an instruction or request before finding another strategy.

*People always make the best choices available to them
at the time*

Someone who is wasted makes choices, often terrible, but the best available in their cloud of confusion. Someone blinded with grief might make angry, irrational, defiant choices. Someone limited by ignorance makes the best ignorant choices they can. Seemingly vicious casting directors are functioning with narrow resources. People do not set out to make a bad decision any more than filmmakers, as is often repeated, "set out to make a bad movie." Our penal system fails disastrously because incarceration is about punishment rather than teaching those who have failed to have better choices available to them. This presupposition is a way of giving everybody a break, the benefit of the doubt and a second chance. As Oprah likes to say "When you know better, you do better."

The map is not the territory

The menu is not the meal. How often have you followed the map carefully arrived at the destination and it was nothing like you expected. We really cannot know reality, but rather our own perceptions of reality. People often respond to their reality map, and there is no right or correct map of the world. Instead, we should each try to create the richest map possible, one that respects the maps of others, while allowing us the greatest number of choices and perspectives.

It is good to assume there is no absolute truth, but merely various perceptions or experiences of it.

Behind every behavior is a positive intention

In class, I ask my students to imagine a derelict, literally lying in a gutter with a bottle in his hand. He finishes off the last dregs of rot-gut booze. What is his positive intention? After a few false starts, someone usually answers "peace" which is right. At that moment it is not his objective to self-destruct, but to quiet the demons in his head and perhaps to fall asleep. In Tennessee

Williams' play the alcoholic character Brick talks about needing to drink until he hears the click in his head. This is important to remember as an actor because objectives should always be stated in the positive in order to be playable. If you think your character is trying to avoid or stop something, always ask what she is therefore trying to achieve or start. As a fellow human being, seeking out the positive intention of someone seemingly pursuing the most outrageously self-destructive behavior is the first step to compassion and even possibly guiding them to find another way to achieve that objective.

Well-formed outcomes

Many actors waste energy on outcomes that are actually dreams, like winning an Oscar or being cast in a Spielberg film. Nothing wrong with dreaming, but these are beyond your control to initiate and to achieve. Even if you launch a brilliant campaign, someone else is still going to decide. Other people, not you, make the call. So outcomes should be formed around what is possible to accomplish.

For big life decisions, such as moving far away, taking on a rigorous training program, a major relationship shift, or radical shift in career choice or strategy, taking the time to examine all desires, resources and consequences is important. While the list below and the form which is Appendix E may seem long, this will actually save time because you will not go down some trail which you never should have traveled in the first place.

Outcome analysis

What do I want?

- An experience I'd like to have?
- A behavior I'd like to change?
- A new skill I hope to develop?
- To feel differently in some situation?
- A destination toward which I can aim my energies?
- Can it be initiated and controlled by me?

- Is it chunked down enough to manageable size?
- Is it stated positively?

When do I want it?

- Have I picked times where it will be appropriate?
- Do I know places and contexts where it will be appropriate?
- Are there times, places and contexts where it is not suitable?
- Are there areas of my life that should be excluded?

How will I know that I have it?

- What will I see, hear and feel inside?
- What will I see, hear and feel around me?
- What pieces might be secured along the way?
- What will things be like once I have had it for a certain period of time?
- What will it be like to look back and review the steps I took to get there?

When I get it, what else in my life will improve?

- Is this part of some other plan?
- Are there residual pay-offs?
- Can I get extra help in maintaining my commitment?
- Is anything at risk?
- What will happen if I don't achieve it?

What resources do I have to help me with this?

- What present abilities will help?
- What physical resources can I employ?
- Are there other people who can aid me?
- Is there extra information, training, shift in attitude or funding I can tap into?

What has stopped me up to now?

- How can I best utilize my resources?
- Which are most useful now?
- Which will be helpful later?
- What are the most effective ways I can ask for help?

What am I going to begin to do now to get what I want?

- What will be the initial step?
- What is something that can be accomplished right now?

What ecology checks will help make sure this change is good for all my system outcomes?

- Any conflicting outcomes? Are there good reasons to preserve the present state and not have the change?
- Incongruence? Are there any contradictions in my VAK perceptions as I describe the outcome?
- Unforeseen loss? What might be lost by having this new behavior?
- Undesired contexts? When would the new behavior be totally inappropriate?
- Unforeseen complications? Will any problem emerge if I have it?
- Parts acknowledgment? Does any part of me object? If so what is the objection?
- Other people? How will those in my life be affected?

Some of these considerations come close to overlapping, but take a slightly different view. Collectively they allow you, if you decide to go ahead, to feel comfortable and confident in doing so.

Content-free process

Should you decide to enroll in NLP certification programs or seek counseling with a therapist trained in NLP processes, one of the big surprises (and some would say great benefits) is that the work is content-free. Or, more accurately, the teacher or counselor does not ask for the details of your situation. You clearly have your own content, but you keep it to yourself. For example, anything that might appear on your self-study form (Appendix A), while a wonderful way to prepare for the training or counseling, remains there. The processes are designed to proceed without participants getting caught in stories or specifics. So if you were to be taken through the Core Transformation discussed earlier, you would not identify the particular behavior you were trying to eliminate or your past traumatic interactions with the part involved, but only share the short answers the part involved gave as you went through the 10-part sequence.

The same is true in my "NLP for Actors" class. Students chose to work on some important and challenging issues in their lives, but they kept this information to themselves. Whether I was guiding all of them, each in their own space or modeling a process with one or two actors, privacy was constant and boundaries always in place. Some of them came to speak with me about their issues privately, asking me to mentor them, but that was always a choice.

Your guide will never know the sordid details, if there are such, and you will be spared the embarrassment of re-hashing them. This would not be for everyone, of course, as there are those who very much wish to share the minute details of trauma, to rant about the SOB who "done them wrong," relive the events for their therapist and/or vent as part of the healing process. They would feel cheated without full disclosure.

But those who would rather not divulge will find the work and guidance clean and respectful. NLP leaders would say that not getting caught in the particulars of the stories frees them to really calibrate the client's breathing, shifts of state, releasing of tension and all the other details that reveal if a significant change is taking place. Grinder maintained that the fact that he and Bandler were not licensed psychotherapists actually helped free and clarify their observations of Satir, Erickson and Perls as NLP was first being created. They could not get caught in the formal processes, traditions or subject matter that might distract them, but were able to isolate words spoken, contact made, shifts in perspective offered, the very elements that the rest of us could emulate once they had codified them. Some would argue that much traditional therapy takes a very long time because there are so many memories to share and details to clarify before even arriving at a plan of action. NLP-based therapy dives right in and, not surprisingly, usually arrives more speedily at resolution. Such therapists also do not dwell on what you don't want (which can take forever), but will proceed swiftly to what you do.

All the processes in this chapter are offered in the hope that they will allow you to stop wasting time and get to it. Acting is such a time-consuming endeavor that just being able to give yourself permission to get around to it can be a great blessing. I found NLP a source of new inspiration and ways to do it. Here's hoping it will give you the same.

Summary

We can move forward by chunking tasks up, down or sideways, depending on whether we need a big-picture perspective, close scrutiny or another take on the situation. In acting, these maneuvers are similar to identifying a character's super-objective, breaking the role down into beats, or abstracting the role to open up other possibilities. In the pursuit of acting employment, it involves going up for career motivation or overall strategy, down for immediate steps to be taken, and sideways for pulling in success energy to a context where failure has occurred. Another fast-track breakthrough process is Core Transformation, where we establish a respectful relationship between the part of ourselves that seems to have been preventing progress, learning and embracing what it really wants for us as a positive intention. Modeling on those who memorize music quickly, a variety of VAK loadings can help in learning lines. Using presuppositions can help productive action and a well-formed outcome strategy can save much time before you actually embark on an important endeavor. NLP training and therapy release clients from embarrassing details in favor of immediate action.

Words/exercises to remember

chunking

content-free process

Core Transformation

memorization strategies

presuppositions

well-formed outcomes

APPENDIX A:
SELF-STUDY FORM

Changes

Times you felt powerless and clueless:

_____

_____

_____

Times you felt totally capable and competent:

_____

_____

_____

Mildly unpleasant memories where you were not at your best:

_____

_____

_____

Mildly pleasant memories where you were at your best:

_____

_____

_____

People with qualities you would really like to emulate:

_____

_____

_____

Something that doesn't really matter any more, but used to matter a lot:

_____

_____

_____

Something from your past that keeps raining on your parade:

_____

_____

_____

Someone you wish to stay in love with or get closer to:

_____

_____

Someone you wish to forget or feel less concerned with:

_____

_____

Changes you would like to make

Internally:

_____

_____

In one-on-one relationships:

_____

_____

In groups:

_____

_____

Symptoms

Habits/addictive behaviors you wish you could break:

_____

_____

Habits you wish you could acquire:

_____

_____

Phobias:

_____

_____

Allergies/repeated illnesses:

_____

_____

Traumatic memories:

_____

_____

Knee-jerk responses:

_____

_____

Circumstances where your buttons get pushed:

_____

_____

Resources

Your most rewarding performances:

_____

_____

Times when you felt fully joyous:

_____

_____

Times when you felt truly inspired:

_____

_____

Times when your comfort zone suddenly greatly expanded:

_____

_____

Things you do as well as anyone:

_____

_____

Things that are easy for you and difficult for others:

_____

_____

Perfect moments you've experienced:

_____

_____

APPENDIX B:
METAPROGRAMS
SELF-ANALYSIS

In what context are you likely to be or employ:

1 PROACTIVE _____
   REACTIVE _____

2 TOWARDS _____
   AWAY   _____

3 INTERNAL _____
   EXTERNAL _____

4 OPTIONS   _____
   PROCEDURES _____

5 GENERAL _____
   SPECIFIC _____

6 MATCH   _____
   MISMATCH _____

Circle the choices in each pair you are more likely to make in most contexts.

Check the one choice you are least likely to make ever.

APPENDIX C: CHARACTER ANALYSIS NLP-STYLE

character _____

actor _____

The character looks like me _____

does not look like me _____

sounds like me _____

does not sound like me _____

feels like me _____

does not feel like me _____

Changes I most need to make are

_____

To my character _____

the world looks _____

the world sounds _____

the world feels, smells, tastes like _____

The most significant impression my character makes in each modality:

V _____

A _____

K _____

My character's primary VAK mode is

_____

Major shifts/synesthesia take place when

_____

_____

_____

META-MODEL tendencies:

1   UNSPECIFIED NOUNS and PRONOUNS
    example(s)   _____

    _____

2   UNSPECIFIED VERBS
    example(s)   _____

    _____

3   NOMINALIZATIONS
    example(s)   _____

    _____

4   POLARITY WORDS
    example(s)   _____

    _____

5   MIND READING
    example(s)   _____

    _____

CORE STATES
(circle ones achieved, X out those most often out of reach)
beingness   okay-ness   peacefulness   lovingness   oneness

METAPROGRAMS (circle pattern tendencies)
1 proactive/reactive   2 towards/away   3 internal/external
4 options/procedures   5 general/specific   6 match/mismatch

RAPPORT

My character and the other are most in rapport when

_____

_____

_____

are least in rapport when

_____

_____

_____

As actors, we need to be most in rapport when

_____

_____

_____

The positive intentions behind my character's most reprehensible behavior are

_____

_____

_____

If I could NLP my character, I would

_____

_____

_____

APPENDIX D: FINDING ANCHORS IN THE SCENE

Ask yourself which anchors may be present in:

architectural elements   _____

furniture   _____

hand props   _____

clothing   _____

jewelry   _____

grooming   _____

facial expressions   _____

gestures   _____

movements   _____

physical proximity or touch _____

sounds   _____

non-verbals   _____

words or phrases   _____

tone of voice   _____

timing   _____

Try to find at least one positive and one negative anchor in

1 the acting space

_____

_____

2 your partner's physical behavior

_____

_____

3 what your partner says or how she says it

_____

_____

4 Try to find for each character a moment when a new anchoring takes place during the scene itself

_____

_____

You may wish to share some anchors you have discovered in the scene, but then keep others to yourself, just as the character would.

APPENDIX E:
OUTCOME FORM

1   What do you want?

_____

_____

_____

Your present unwanted state

_____

Circumstances under which it occurs

_____

How is it cued or triggered?

_____

Future desired state

_____

2   How will you know when you have it? What will you:

see?   _____

hear?   _____

feel?   _____

timing _____

3   Contexts in which you want it?
    Where?   _____
    When?   _____
    With whom?   _____
    Under what circumstances do you *not* want it?

    _____

4   What will having it do for you?

5   When you achieve it, what else in your life will improve?

6   How will having it affect other areas of your life?
    Does any part object?   _____
    What will be added?   _____
    What taken away?   _____
    What is worth saving?   _____
    Are there any residual benefits from the old way?

    _____

    When you get it, will anything be at risk?

    _____

7   What resources do you need to get it?

    _____
    _____
    _____

8   What resources do you already have to help you?

    _____
    _____
    _____

9   What other ways are there to get it?

    _____
    _____
    _____

10 What will happen if you don't get it?

_____

_____

_____

11 What has stopped you from already having it?

_____

_____

_____

What would have been lost if you had made the change back then?

_____

_____

_____

12 What is a first step you can take to begin achieving this now?

_____

_____

_____

13 Imagine yourself in the future, having your outcome. look back and determine what steps you took to achieve what you now have

_____

_____

_____

APPENDIX F:
SAMPLE CLASS SYLLABUS
AND SCHEDULE

If you choose to offer a class based on NLP, you will of course want to find your own way of adding this adjunct to your core acting curriculum. I am offering my course materials just as a sample. I am glad to mentor you if you choose to contact me: barton@uoregon.edu.

Syllabus for NLP for actors

An introduction to applying principles of Neuro-Linguistic Programming to the acting process and to communication among theatre artists and others.

Text

Acting Reframes by Robert Barton

Objectives

To offer alternative ways of approaching and developing characterization, doing character analysis, rehearsing and meeting performance challenges, filtered through perspectives offered by NLP. To accomplish a high level of personal growth and communication skills, in theatre situations and beyond the theatre.

Attendance

Any absence beyond two lowers the final grade one full letter. Being late for class three times constitutes an absence. Missing coaching sessions and conferences constitutes absences. Always contact the instructor and anyone with whom you are partnered in a project if you will be absent or late.

Tentative major assignments

- Developing monologs in various modalities
- Creating an original "Best Day of My Life" monolog
- Scene work
- Midterm showcase and preparation
- Variety of self-analysis and character analysis
- Open-ended final project

Grades

In a class like this, excellence of effort is expected and an A is yours to lose. This could be done by excessive latenesses, absences where I am not notified, failing to take part in discussion, to turn in observations on time, to be off book on deadline, or in some way dropping the ball enough times to chip away at the grade. Everyone should achieve an A and it is my hope that all will. And I welcome your checking with me.

Final projects

Will be individual original works 15–20 minutes in length scheduled for the last week of the term and our final meeting. It may be primarily a performance, guided activity or a lecture/demonstration. It is never too early to start pondering possibilities. Here are some:

- Using NLP to deal with a major experience, such as grief or a major move.
- Applying NLP to a particular form of theatre, e.g. guerrilla theatre or improv company work.

- Monologs demonstrating VAK in a particular profession/ activity, such as V, A and K evangelical preachers or addicted gamers.
- Satiric NLP guides, such as non-core states, unrapport and unframing.
- A monolog in which the character commits every NLP *faux pas* possible or perhaps demonstrates before and after being NLPed.
- Results of investigating any aspect we have only hit on lightly, such as anchoring or chunking.
- NLP guide for surviving in a particular job or subculture, such as being a receptionist, a pizza delivery person or a sorority sister.
- An NLP guide for traveling or surviving in a particular country or region.
- Adapting a classic fairy tale or myth with NLP components.
- A guided meditation, helping classmates unearth particular memories or resources, establishing a desired mood, and/or preparing for an upcoming performance challenge.

NOTE: Some of the more exciting and valuable projects have been designed for a particular target group so the presenter is using this class session to rehearse for that projected event and the class role-plays the targeted population. These are particularly rewarding because they have a life and make a contribution past this class.

Circumstances

This is an advanced class by application, requiring the instructor's permission to register. I limit admission to 16 students. When the time comes for scene work, I assign scenes with two different sets of partners working on the same scene and all scenes being worked on having the same basic set. This allows quick transitions between various couples working onstage with no need for additional set up; it also allows two actors to share insights as they both work on a character, and invites rehearsal experiments coming out of that familiarity. I assign the entire text within the first few weeks, so that we can jump around as the needs of the group emerge and return to material, if more exposure seems warranted.

I try to find a current film that the class can attend (individually rather than as a field trip), analyze and discuss regarding NLP. In winter 2010 it was *Up in the Air*, which has one major character who is highly visual and unskilled in rapport and another who is auditory/kinesthetic and gifted in rapport. It also has numerous examples of reframing.

Schedule

This sample schedule is for a class that meets three times a week, each meeting lasting just under two hours, for a ten-week quarter period. At University of Oregon, class periods are 50 minutes long. This class meets 10–10:50 at which time there is a 10-minute break and reconvenes 11:00–11:50, with some variation.

Each class opens with one warm-up, or a combination of the warm-ups in Chapter 4, followed by an Open Frame discussion. On Day 1 this covers initial questions students have regarding NLP and after that a chance to share what they are noticing as they increase their exposure and knowledge of it. Warm-ups take about 10 minutes and Open Frame 5–10 more. Because they occur each period, they are not noted in the schedule below.

Week 1

DAY 1

- Discussion of NLP definitions, history, basic principles
- Assign Chs 1 and 2
- Trunk-packing exercise and de-brief

DAY 2

- Learning VAK through repetition of self-descriptions
- Assign Ch. 3 and warm-up section of Ch. 4

- Film we might watch (this term *Up in the Air*)
- Review – VAK What am I?

    - Strong suits and weaknesses
    - Eye access cues

- Set up "Best Day of My Life" assignment
- Submodalities exercises
- VAK arguments
- Assign 1 line in each modality

DAY 3

- Assign Chs 4 and 5
- Share 1 line in each modality
- Rapport checklist
- Assign in and out of rapport discussions
- Metaprograms
- Try something else: assign dragging roommate assignment

(This is a challenge assignment, taking the almost universal experience of having one roommate who does not pick after himself, do his dishes etc. Class members each try to come up with a persuasive strategy using NLP language and tools to get the errant roommate to start carrying his weight in apartment and relationship maintenance)

- Transformative vocabulary
- Assign and work VAK actor/directors

Week 2

DAY 4

- Discuss assigned film from NLP perspective
- Try something else – messy roommate situation reports
- Review rapport list, self-analysis
- Review transformative vocabulary
- Side coach submodality adjustments

- Assign Ch. 6
- VAK arguments, same, then different
  (planning party, planning vacation, redecorating, picking out a new pet)
- Partner work, practicing levels of:

    - In rapport, complete agreement (topic – how great NLP is)
    - Out of rapport, complete disagreement (topic – controversial new building on campus)
    - In rapport, complete disagreement (topic – success record of affirmative action)
    - Out of rapport, complete agreement (topic – Method acting)

- Introduce and assign metaprograms
- Assign VAK directors, actors, hosts for TV show with famous guests

(To make this more fun for the hosts, I meet with them to develop two totally different shows and host personalities, one somewhat fawning and touchy feely, the other snarky and embittered)

- Coach "Best Day" monolog with partners

- Submodality coaching, debrief
- Prep, time, then present and critique "Best Day" monologs
- Assign Timmys, Suzannes (V, A, K and synthesthetic)

Week 3

- Discuss emerging field of positive psychology, relation to NLP
- Set up and present VAK TV shows

DAY 8

- Discuss and demonstrate phone rapport
- Discuss cultures and their tendencies to VAK
- Present and critique Timmy, Suzanne speeches
- Learn anchoring

DAY 9

- Piece of Cake exercise
- Discuss positive anchor stacking and resources

Week 4

DAY 10

- VAK – what makes each a good friend?
- Discuss outcomes vs. goals (and possible blends – "outgoals") (examples: letters students wrote to selves to be sent a year later [who was happy and who not when they arrived?])
  - importance of getting all theatre faculty to know you and have positive impression of me
- Continue Timmy and Suzanne presentations

DAY 11

- "Best Day" repeats, with copies turned in

DAY 12

- Memorization strategies
- Review chunking
- Explore non-verbals
- Scenes assigned, rehearsal time

Week 5

DAY 13

• Coaching VAK and Timmy/Suzanne monologs

DAY 14

• Coaching VAK and Timmy/Suzanne monologs

DAY 15

• VAK and Timmy/Suzanne repeats

Week 6

DAY 16

• Chunking exercises

DAY 17

• Scene coaching

DAY 18

• Memorization strategies implemented, rehearsal time

Week 7

DAY 19

• Partners switch scenes
  (Actors are not warned about this. They arrive in class
  expecting to present with the partners with whom they have
  been rehearsing, but do so with the other actor who has been

working on their partner's role. No prep. time. Full use of all NLP skills, maximum calibration)
- Explore final project ideas
- Assign key searching

DAY 20

- Review NLP character analysis
- Partner warm-ups
- Share key choices

DAY 21

- NLP institute, certification and other further study
- Individual conferences to brainstorm final projects

Week 8

DAY 22

- Review congruence
- Turn in/discuss character analysis
- Meet with partner over anchors in scene
- Rehearsal exercises: Handicaps, Moment before, Half hour before
- Set up Shadowing for Wed.
- Teach Circle of Excellence
- Set up interview unit, forms

DAY 23

- Discuss, further explore anchors
- Turn in interview forms (Actors select a job they actually want or make up a context in which they would like to work)
- Shadowing scenes

DAY 24

- Discuss when to use Piece of Cake, when Circle of Excellence
- Role reversal exercise

Week 9

DAY 25

- Check in on final projects
- Interview workshop
  (I role-play a first-level interviewer for a large employment agency, so that I can interview half the class, sitting in a semi-circle, all at once)

DAY 26

- Neutral mask work
- Other rehearsal exercises: role reversal, contact every line, object passing

DAY 27

- Core Transformation

Week 10

DAY 28

- Diagnostic rehearsal exercises (selected based on where actors seem to need the most work)

DAY 29

- Final scene presentations and critiques
  (While scenes have been shared in numerous forms, this is the first time the entire scene is presented with actual originally assigned scene partners)

DAY 30

- First round of final projects

Exam period

- Complete presentation of final projects

GLOSSARY

NLP has generated quite a bit of lingo. I have tried to keep it at a minimum in this volume. Nevertheless if you decide to study more, you will run into an abundance of terminology for which the list below may be a helpful resource.

Accessing cues Behaviors used within any representational system; e.g. eye movements, voice tones, postures, breathing, etc.

Anchor A cue or trigger that elicits a response, similar to the stimulus–response of classical conditioning.

Associated Being in an experience or memory as fully and completely as possible with all the senses engaged.

Auditory The representational system based on hearing the world.

Backtrack To review or summarize aloud information you have recently elicited, usually for rapport and to invite revision or correction.

Behavioral flexibility The ability to vary one's behavior in order to elicit a desired response from another person (in contrast to repeating a behavior that hasn't worked).

Break state To change a person's state dramatically. Usually used to pull someone out of an unpleasant state.

Calibrate To effectively "read" another person's responses and adjust accordingly.

Channel One of the five senses.

Chunking   Shifting the size of the object, situation or experience being considered. This can be altered by chunking up to a more general category, chunking down to a more specific category, or chunking sideways or laterally to others of the same type or class.

Collapsing anchors   See: Stacking anchors.

Congruent   When all of a person's internal strategies, behaviors and parts are in agreement and working together coherently.

Context   The surrounding within which a communication or response occurs. The context is one of the cues that elicit specific responses.

Context reframing   Placing a problematic response in a different context that gives it a new and different – usually more positive – meaning.

Conversational postulates   Questions which only ask for a yes/no answer but which typically elicit a behavioral response; e.g. "Can you shut the door?"

Critical submodalities   The submodalities which are most powerful in determining a person's response.

Cross-over mirroring   Matching a person but with a different type of behavior; e.g. pacing breathing with hand movement.

Dissociated   Experiencing an event or memory from a perspective other than seeing it out of your own eyes.

Dovetail   To fit together more than one outcome, story, etc.

Driver   The most crucial submodality in a given context; changing it automatically changes many other submodalities and "drives" the response. See: Critical submodalities.

Ecology   Considering the effects of a change on the larger system instead of on just one isolated behavior, part, or person.

Embedded command   Nesting a command in a sentence so that it is grammatically not a command but really is. "It might be worthwhile considering how to do that!"

Eye accessing cues   Movements of a person's eyes that indicate the representational system being used or sought.

Firing an anchor   Repeating the overt behavior that triggers a certain response.

First position   See: Self-referential index.

Flexibility   Having more than one behavioral choice in a situation.

Future-pace   Rehearsing in all systems so that a specific behavior will occur naturally and automatically in future situations.

Generative intervention   An intervention that solves a single problem and also generates other changes that make the person's life better in many other ways. (Contrast with: Remedial intervention.)

Gustatory   The sense of taste.

Hallucination   An internal representation of, or about, the world that has no basis in present sensory experience.

Incongruent   When two or more of a person's representations, parts, or programs are in conflict.

Installation   Teaching or acquiring a new strategy or behavior, generally by rehearsal or future-pacing.

Kinesthetic   The sense of feeling. May be subdivided into: tactile feelings (Kt); internal body sensations (Kp); and emotional responses or meta-feelings (Km).

Lead system   The representational system initially used to access stored information, such as making a visual image of a friend in order to get the feeling of liking him/her.

Leading   Guiding another person in a specific direction.

Lost performative   A linguistic pattern in which the person performing the action or judgment is missing from the sentence.

Map of reality   A person's perception of events.

Matching   See: Mirroring, Pacing.

Meaning reframing   Ascribing a new meaning to a behavior/response without changing the context.

Meta-model   A set of language patterns that focuses attention on how people delete, distort, generalize, limit or specify their realities. It provides a series of questions useful for recovering lost or unspecified information, and for loosening rigid patterns of thinking.

Meta-outcome   The outcome of the outcome: one that is more general and basic than the stated one; e.g. "getting my self-respect back" is the meta-outcome of "insulting that person."

Meta-person   The observer in an exercise, who has the task of giving sensory feedback to the programmer (and sometimes also to the person in the "client" role) in order to improve performance.

Metaphor   A story, parable or analogy that relates one situation, experience or phenomenon to another.

Milton-model   A set of indirect language patterns useful for delivering a message in such a way that the person readily accepts it and responds to it.

Mirroring   Matching one's behavior to that of another person, usually to establish rapport, preparatory to leading or intervening.

Modal operators   Mode of operating, one or more of four broad categories of acting: desire, possibility, necessity, choice. A modal operator always indicates incongruence. In total congruence, all four modal operators collapse together.

Modality   One of the senses. See: Representational systems.

Modeling   Observing and specifying how something happens, or how someone thinks or behaves, and then demonstrating the process for others so that they can learn to do it.

Nest   To fit one thing (outcome, story, etc.) within another.

New behavior generator   A step-by-step process for selecting and installing specific new responses and behaviors in response to contexts that have been problematic in the past.

Nominalization   Words which result from the process of taking actions (verbs) and converting them into things (nouns) which actually have no existence as things; e.g. you can't put them in a wheelbarrow. Examples: are "love," "freedom," "happiness," "respect," "frustration."

Observer   A dissociated meta-position from which you can observe or review events, seeing yourself and others interact.

Olfactory   The sense of smell.

Organ language   Idioms that refer to specific body parts or activities; e.g. "Get off my back," "pain in the neck," etc.

Outcome   Desired result.

Pacing   Matching or mirroring another person's nonverbal and/or verbal behavior. Useful for gaining rapport, preparatory to leading or intervening. See: Mirroring.

Parts   Different facets of a person's behaviors, strategies, programs, personality; the "parts" that want you to be safe, independent, in control, loved, respected, spiritual, etc.

Perceptual filter   An attitude, point of view, perspective or set of assumptions or presuppositions about the object, person or situation.

Polarity response   A response which reverses, negates or takes the opposite position of a previous statement.

Predicates   Process words: words that express action or relationship with respect to a subject (verbs, adverbs and adjectives). The words may reflect the representational system being used or they may be non-specific.

Preferred representational system   The representational system which a person habitually uses to process information or experiences; usually the one in which the person can make the most detailed distinctions.

Process words   See: Predicates.

Rapport   A condition in which responsiveness has been established, often described as feeling safe or trusting, or willing.

Reframing   A process by which a person's perception of a specific event or behavior is altered, resulting in a different response. Sometimes subdivided into "context reframing," "meaning reframing" and "six-step reframing."

Remedial intervention   An intervention that only solves the specific immediate problem. (Contrast with: Generative intervention.)

Representational systems   The internal representations of experience: seeing (visual), hearing (auditory), feeling (kinesthetic).

Resource state   The experience of a useful response: an ability, attitude, behavior, characteristic, perspective or quality that is useful in some context.

Second position   Experiencing an event from the perspective of the person you are encountering.

Secondary gain The positive intention or desired outcome (often obscure or unknown) of an undesired or problem behavior.

Sensory acuity The ability to make sensory discriminations to identify distinctions between different states or events.

Sensory-based Information which is correlated with what has been received by the senses. (Contrast with: Hallucination.)

Self-referential index Experiencing the world from your own perspective; being associated into yourself.

Separator state Eliciting a neutral state between two other states to prevent them from combining or connecting with each other.

Shift referential index To take only the perspective of someone else, while keeping your own criteria with which to evaluate and respond to events.

Six-step reframing A complex process in which an undesirable behavior is metaphorically separated from the desired outcome of the "part" generating the behavior, so that the "part" can more easily adopt new behaviors that satisfy its positive intention and that do not have the undesirable side effects of the original behavior.

Sorting polarities Separating tendencies or "parts" that pull a person in opposite directions into cleanly defined and organized entities, preparatory to integration at the level of outcomes.

Stacking anchors Using the same anchor for a number of resources, integrating them.

State A state of being, or a condition of body/mind response or experience at a particular moment.

Stimulus–response The repeated association between an experience and a particular response (Pavlovian conditioning) such that the stimulus becomes a trigger or cue for the response.

Strategy A sequence of mental and behavioral representations which lead to a specific outcome.

Submodalities The smaller elements within a representational system; e.g. a visual image can be bright, dim, clear, fuzzy, moving, still, large, small, etc.

Swish   A generative submodalities pattern used to change habits and responses.

Switch referential index   To "become" someone else fully by taking both the perspective and the criteria and history, etc. of someone else.

Synesthesia   A very close and quick overlap between a sequence of two or more representational systems such as "see/feel" (feelings overlap with what is seen) or "hear/feel" (feelings overlap with what is heard).

Tag questions   Negative questions tagged onto the end of a sentence in order to diffuse polarity responses; e.g. "don't you?" "can't you?" "aren't you?", etc.

Tape-editing   A process of reviewing past behavior and then selecting and rehearsing or future-pacing new behavior and responses in order to alter future responses in similar situations. See: New behavior generator.

Third position   See: Observer.

Transderivational search   Searching back through one's memories to find experiences that are similar in some way – usually in feeling response. Often used to identify important early formative experiences that continue to affect the person so that they can be changed.

Translating   The process of rephrasing words from one representational system into another, useful in bridging understanding between two people.

Universal quantifier   A linguistic term for words which are applied to all cases and all situations without exception; e.g. "all," "every," "always" and negations such as "never," "none," etc.

Visual   The representational system based on seeing.

FURTHER STUDY/
BIBLIOGRAPHY

The best way to study more NLP is without question to seek out an institute and register for a workshop. Most offer brief introductory sessions of a few hours, specialized workshops over a few days, and longer certification programs at various levels. The basic NLP Certified Practitioner program is anywhere from 21 to 30 days, which may be a few consecutive weeks or spread over eight months of long weekends. I recommend the latter. I found it tremendously useful after three full days of immersion in "new NLPing" to be able to go back home, contemplate and apply what I had learned before jumping back into the fray the following month.

Supplies

The most thorough single U.S. source for ordered materials is NLP Comprehensive, 4895 Riverbend Road, Boulder, CO 80301-2640, 1-800-233-1657, www.nipco.com (audiotapes, DVDs, CDs, videotapes, books, home study guides, discount packs, training, certification and conference information, plus a DVD rental club service). In the U.K., the most comprehensive source of publications is probably MX Publishing U.K., 335 Princess Park Manor, Royal Drive, London N11 3GX, 02895 811172, www.mxpublishing.co.uk, enquiry@mxpublishing.co.uk.

Recommended books

There are a huge number of books available, many alas almost incomprehensible and none of which relate NLP to theatre. For a more extensive introductory exposure to the field, here are what I consider some of the best places to start reading:

Andreas, Connirae and Andreas, Tamora, *Core Transformation.* Fort Worth: Harcourt, Brace, Jovanovich, 1995.

Linden, Anne, *Mindworks: An Introduction to NLP*. Carmarthen, Wales and Bethel, CT: Crown House Publishing, 2008.

O'Connor, Joseph and Seymour, John. *Introducing NLP.* London: Element, 2002.

Ready, Romilla and Burton, Kate, *Neuro-linguistic Programming for Dummies.* Chichester: John Wiley, 2004.

Vaknin, Shlomo, *NLP for Beginners: Only the Essentials.* Inner Patch Publishing, 2009.

Articles

Barton, Robert, "Voice in a Visual World," in *The Vocal Vision*. New York: Applause Books, 1998.

Barton, Robert, "Director Modalities," in the "Many Right Ways" column, *Voice and Speech Review*, 1999.

Barton, Robert, "NLP for Actors," in *The Beat* (Acting Forum Journal), 1999.

Barton, Robert, "Actor Modalities," in the "Many Right Ways" column, *Voice and Speech Review*, 2000.

DVDs

Andreas, Connirae, *Core Transformation: A Demonstration with Roger*, 706D-DVD-R, NLP Comprehensive.

Satir, Virginia, *Forgiving Parents*, 729D-DVD-R, NLP Comprehensive.

Andreas, Steve, *Responding to Criticism*, 707D-DVD-R, NLP Comprehensive.

There are numerous DVDs available including entire certification programs, which, while I have not reviewed them, I would approach with great skepticism. The firsthand/hands-on aspect of

NLP training is so crucial that I cannot imagine "getting it" by watching alone.

The most effective DVDs are those focusing on a specific issue, such as the last two above or a single process such as the first.

Web sites highlighting NLP for performers

Rose, David, NLP for Actors – Bring Your Dreams to Life. Available at: www.nlpconnections.com/.../4535-nlp-actors-bring-your-dreams-life.html

Fairley, Molly Ann, Rapid Success with NLP. Available at: www.molly-annfairley.co.uk/index.php/the-arts-nlp.htm

Classic texts

If you decide to immerse yourself in the history and development of the field, you may wish to sample this list:

Andreas, Steve and Faulkner, Charles (eds) *NLP: The New Technology of Achievement*. New York: HarperCollins, 1996.

Bandler, Richard and Grinder, John, *The Structure of Magic I: A Book About Language and Therapy*. Palo Alto, CA: Science and Behavior Books, 1975.

Bandler, Richard and Grinder, John, *Frogs into Princes: Neuro-Linguistic Programming*. Moab, Utah: Real People Press, 1979.

Bandler, Richard and Grinder, John, *Reframing: Neuro-Linguistic Programming and the Transformation of Meaning*. Moab, Utah: Real People Press, 1981.

Bandler, Richard, Andreas, Steve and Andreas, Connirae (eds) *Using Your Brain – for a Change*. Moab, Utah: Real People Press, 1985.

Dilts, Robert B., *Changing Belief Systems with NLP*. Palo Alto, CA: Meta Publications, 1990.

Dilts, Robert B. and Epstein, Todd, *Tools for Dreamers: Strategies for Creativity*. Palo Alto, CA: Meta Publications, 1991.

Dilts, Robert B., Hallborn, Tim and Smith, Suzi, *Beliefs: Pathways to Health and Well-being*. Portland, Oregon: Metamorphous Press,1990.

Grinder, John and Bandler, Richard, *The Structure of Magic II: A Book About Communication and Change*. Palo Alto, CA: Science and Behavior Books, 1975.

Grinder, John and Bandler, Richard, *Patterns of the Hypnotic Techniques of Milton H. Erickson, Volume 1*. Portland, Oregon: Metamorphous Press,1997.

O'Connor, Joseph and McDermott, Ian, *Principles of NLP*. London: Thorsons, 1996.

Satir, Virginia, Grinder, John and Bandler, Richard, *Changing with Families: A Book about Further Education for Being Human*. Palo Alto, CA: Science and Behavior Books, 1976.

INDEX